# Pellet Grill Cookbook

*150 Easy-to-Make Pellet Smoker Recipes
for the Best Barbeque*

*Dave Bolton*

Published by Northern Press Inc.

# Contents

# Introduction

Barbecuing can be difficult work. You have to deal with dangerous fires, dirty coals, hot embers, not to mention a lot of time and TLC. But what you get from all of this is rewarding. You get savory and succulent smoke-infused meals that you couldn't get without all of that time and hard work.

The wood pellet grills of today offer the convenience of electric smokers with several other benefits. These benefits include higher temperature options, no wasted fuel, no soot, and real wood-generated cooking heat. The pellets are free from moisture, which you can't get from wet or green wood.

Smoking has long been used to preserve meats. In fact, smoking helped to increase food safety and prevent diseases. When modern food preservation methods came to be, smoking as a means of preservation become obsolete, and people started smoking more for the taste, texture, and cultural value. Still, smoking is used for preservation in some underdeveloped nations.

Pellet grills are the latest step in the smoking tradition. Maybe you just got your pellet grill and you are dying to try it out, or you may have had yours for a while now and you just want some new recipes. Either way, this book has you covered.

# Beef

# Almond Crusted Beef Fillet

## Ingredients:

- ❖ ¼ c. chopped almonds
- ❖ One T. Dijon mustard
- ❖ One c. chicken broth
- ❖ Salt
- ❖ 1/3 c. chopped onion
- ❖ ¼ c. olive oil
- ❖ Pepper
- ❖ Two T. curry powder
- ❖ 3 pounds beef fillet tenderloin

## Instructions:

i. Rub the pepper and salt into the tenderloin.

ii. Place the almonds, mustard, chicken broth, curry, onion, and olive oil into a bowl. Stir well to combine.

iii. Take this mixture and rub the tenderloin generously with it.

iv. Add wood pellets to your smoker and follow your cooker's startup procedure. Preheat your smoker, with your lid closed, until it reaches 450.

v. Lay on the grill, cover, and smoke for ten minutes on both sides.

vi. Continue to cook until it reaches your desired doneness.

vii. Take it off the grill and let it rest for at least ten minutes.

**Servings| 4**          **Time required: 55 minutes**

# Bacon Cheese Steak Meatloaf

## Ingredients:

- ❖ Two chopped garlic cloves
- ❖ One chopped poblano chile
- ❖ One chopped medium onion
- ❖ One T. canola oil
- ❖ Two pounds extra lean ground beef
- ❖ ½ c. tiger sauce
- ❖ Two c. breadcrumbs
- ❖ One beaten egg
- ❖ Two c. shredded Swiss Cheese
- ❖ One T. A1 Steak sauce
- ❖ ½ pound cooked and crumbled bacon
- ❖ Two T. Montreal steak seasoning

## Instructions:

i.   Using a pan on stove top, add in the oil and heat before adding the poblano, onion, and garlic. Allow these veggies to cook for three to five minutes, or until the onion has become just barely translucent.

ii.  Add wood pellets to your smoker and follow your cooker's startup procedure. Preheat your smoker, with your lid closed, until it reaches 225.

iii. Place the cooked veggies in a bowl along with the breadcrumbs, egg, Swiss cheese, bacon, steak sauce, steak seasoning, and ground beef. Make sure that you use your hands to mix everything together.

They will do a better job than a spoon will. Once everything is very well incorporated, form it into a loaf shape.

iv.   Place the meatloaf in a cast iron skillet and set this on the grill. Lower the lid on your grill and allow the meatloaf to smoke for two hours. The meat is completely cooked once it has reached 165.

v.    Once your meatloaf is cooked through, brush on the tiger sauce and take it off the grill and allow this to rest for ten minutes before you serve the meatloaf.

**Servings| 8-10**                          **Time required: 2 hours**

# Herbed Beef Eye Fillet

## Ingredients:

- ❖ Pepper
- ❖ Salt
- ❖ Two T. chopped rosemary
- ❖ Two T. chopped basil
- ❖ Two T. olive oil
- ❖ 3 cloves crushed garlic
- ❖ ¼ c. chopped oregano
- ❖ ¼ c. chopped parsley
- ❖ Two pounds beef eye fillet

## Instructions:

i. Use salt and pepper to rub in the meat before placing in a container.

ii. Place the garlic, oil, rosemary, oregano, basil, and parsley in a bowl. Stir well to combine.

iii. Rub the fillet generously with this mixture on all sides. Allow the meat to sit on the counter for 30 minutes.

iv. Add wood pellets to your smoker and follow your cooker's startup procedure. Preheat your smoker, with your lid closed, until it reaches 450.

v. Lay the meat on the grill, cover, and smoke for ten minutes per side or your preferred tenderness.

vi. Once it is done to your likeness, allow it to rest for ten minutes. Slice and enjoy.

**Servings| 6**          **Time required: 8 hours**

# Balsamic Vinegar Molasses Steak

## Ingredients:

- ❖ Pepper
- ❖ Salt
- ❖ One T. balsamic vinegar
- ❖ Two T. molasses
- ❖ One T. red wine vinegar
- ❖ One c. beef broth
- ❖ Two and one-half pounds steak of choice

## Instructions:

i.   Lay the steaks in a zip top bag.

ii.  Add the balsamic vinegar, red wine vinegar, molasses, and beef broth to a bowl. Combine thoroughly by stirring.

iii. On the top of the steaks, drizzle this mixture.

iv.  Place into the refrigerator for eight hours.

v.   Add wood pellets to your smoker and follow your cooker's startup procedure. Preheat your smoker, with your lid closed, until it reaches 350.

vi.  Take the steaks out of the refrigerator 30 minutes before you are ready to grill.

vii. Place on the grill, cover, and smoke for ten mins. per side, or until meat is tender.

viii. Place onto plates and let them rest ten minutes.

**Servings| 4**                    **Time required: 8 hours 50 minutes**

# Herbed Steaks

## Ingredients:

- ❖ Pinch red pepper flakes
- ❖ ½ t. coriander seeds
- ❖ Two t. green peppercorns
- ❖ Two t. black peppercorns
- ❖ Two T. chopped mint leaves
- ❖ ¼ c. olive oil
- ❖ Two T. peanut oil
- ❖ 3 pounds flank steak

## Instructions:

i. Sprinkle the flank steak with salt and rub generously. Lay the meat in a large zip-top bag.

ii. Mix together the red pepper flakes, coriander, peppercorns, mint leaves, olive oil, and peanut oil.

iii. Pour this mixture over the flank steak.

iv. Place into the refrigerator for four hours.

v. Add wood pellets to your smoker and follow your cooker's startup procedure. Preheat your smoker, with your lid closed, until it reaches 450.

vi. Take the flank steak out of the refrigerator 30 minutes before you are ready to grill it.

vii. Place the flank steak onto the grill and grill ten minutes on each. You can grill longer if you want the steak more well-done.

viii.    After removing from the grill and set for about ten mins. Slice before serving.

**Servings| 6**                          **Time required: 5 hours 40 minutes**

# Beer Honey Steaks

## Ingredients:

- ❖ Pepper
- ❖ Juice of one lemon
- ❖ One c. beer of choice
- ❖ One T. honey
- ❖ Salt
- ❖ Two T. olive oil
- ❖ One t. thyme
- ❖ 4 steaks of choice

## Instructions:

i.    Season the steaks with pepper and salt.

ii.   Mix together the olive oil, lemon juice, honey, thyme, and beer.

iii.  Rub the steaks with this mixture generously.

iv.   Add wood pellets to your smoker and follow your cooker's startup procedure. Preheat your smoker, with your lid closed, until it reaches 450.

v.    Place the steaks onto the grill, cover, and smoke for ten mins. per side.

vi.   For about 10 mins, let it cool after removing from the grill.

**Servings| 4**                    **Time required: 55 minutes**

# La Rochelle Steak

## *Ingredients:*

- ❖ One T. red currant jelly
- ❖ ½ t. salt
- ❖ 3 t. curry powder
- ❖ 8 oz. pineapple chunks in juice
- ❖ 1 ½ pounds flank steak
- ❖ ¼ c. olive oil

## *Instructions:*

i.   Put the flank steak into a large bag.

ii.  Mix the pepper, salt, red currant jelly, curry powder, pineapple chunks with juice, and olive oil together.

iii. Pour this mixture over the flank steak.

iv.  Place into the refrigerator for four hours.

v.   Add wood pellets to your smoker and follow your cooker's startup procedure. Preheat your smoker, with your lid closed, until it reaches 350.

vi.  When you are ready to cook the steak, remove steak from refrigerator 30 minutes before ready to cook.

vii. Lay the steaks on the grill, cover, and smoke for ten minutes on both sides, or done to your liking.

viii. Remove from grill and allow to cool for about ten minutes.

**Servings| 4**                    **Time required: 5 hours**

# Fennel and Thyme Veal Shoulder

## Ingredients:

- ❖ Pepper
- ❖ Two T. thyme
- ❖ 4 T. olive oil
- ❖ Two T. chopped thyme
- ❖ One thinly sliced fennel bulb
- ❖ Salt
- ❖ 3 ½ pound veal shoulder roast

## Instructions:

i.   Sprinkle the roast with pepper and salt and rub generously.

ii.  In a bowl, put the oil, wine, fennel, thyme, pepper, and salt. Stir well to combine.

iii. Rub the roast generously on all sides with this mixture.

iv.  Add wood pellets to your smoker and follow your cooker's startup procedure. Preheat your smoker, with your lid closed, until it reaches 450.

v.   Cover after placing in the grill. For about 25 mins., cook the meat.

vi.  Take the roast off the grill and take an internal temperature. It should be no lower than 130.

vii. Slice and serve.

**Servings| 8**            **Time required: 55 minutes**

# Lemony Mustard Crusted Veal

## Ingredients:

- ❖ Pepper
- ❖ Salt
- ❖ ¼ c. breadcrumbs
- ❖ Two T. water
- ❖ One t. basil
- ❖ One pound veal round roast
- ❖ One T. Dijon mustard
- ❖ One T. lemon juice
- ❖ One t. thyme

## Instructions:

i.   Lay the roast in a shallow roasting pan on a rack.

ii.  Mix together the pepper, thyme, basil, lemon juice, mustard, water, and breadcrumbs.

iii. Spread this mixture over the roast being sure to get all sides.

iv.  Add wood pellets to your smoker and follow your cooker's startup procedure. Preheat your smoker, with your lid closed, until it reaches 450.

v.   Place the roast onto the grill and cook for ten minutes per side until it is to your desired doneness.

vi.  Take off from the grill and allow to set for ten minutes.

**Servings| 8**            **Time required: 2 ½ Hours**

# Classic Burger

## Ingredients:

- ❖ Pepper
- ❖ Salt
- ❖ One chopped onion
- ❖ ½ pound ground pork
- ❖ One T. chopped parsley
- ❖ 4 T. olive oil
- ❖ 1 ¼ pounds ground beef
- ❖ Toppings of choice

## Instructions:

i.   Mix together all of the ingredients, except the toppings.

ii.  Use your hands and mix the ingredients well until everything is thoroughly combined. Form into six patties.

iii. Place into the refrigerator for 30 minutes.

iv.  Add wood pellets to your smoker and follow your cooker's startup procedure. Preheat your smoker, with your lid closed, until it reaches 425.

v.   Grill the burgers, covered, for four minutes on each side.

vi.  Serve with toppings of your choice.

**Servings| 6**                    **Time required: One hour**

# Green Burgers

## Ingredients:

- ❖ Pepper
- ❖ Two pounds ground beef
- ❖ One T. chopped cilantro
- ❖ One egg
- ❖ One pound frozen spinach, thawed and drained
- ❖ 3 cloves garlic
- ❖ 3 T. olive oil
- ❖ One T. chopped tarragon
- ❖ Salt
- ❖ Two chopped green onions

## Instructions:

i. Wash and chop the green onion. Mix the onion and spinach together.

ii. Add in the salt, pepper, cilantro, tarragon, oil, egg, garlic, and ground beef.

iii. Use your hands and mix the ingredients until everything is thoroughly combined. Shape into six burgers.

iv. Add wood pellets to your smoker and follow your cooker's startup procedure. Preheat your smoker, with your lid closed, until it reaches 380.

v. Cover the burgers after placing on the grill. Both sides should be cooked for 5 mins.

vi. Serve with toppings of choice.

**Servings| 6                     Time required: 35 minutes**

# Stuffed Peppers

## Ingredients:

- ❖ One T. garlic, minced
- ❖ One large diced onion
- ❖ 1.5 c. grated cheddar, divided
- ❖ One t. pepper
- ❖ 14-ounce can tomato paste
- ❖ One t. seasoned salt
- ❖ ½ pound sausage
- ❖ ½ pound ground beef
- ❖ One poblano chile, seeded and chopped
- ❖ 4 large bell peppers, seeds, top, and core removed

## Instructions:

i.    Lay the peppers inside of a disposable aluminum pan. If they won't stay upright on their own, you can wrap a foil ring around their base to keep them standing.

ii.   Add wood pellets to your smoker and follow your cooker's startup procedure. Preheat your smoker, with your lid closed, until it reaches 350.

iii.  Using the stovetop, heat a large pan. Brown the sausage and the beef for five to seven minutes. Drain the fat and crumble up the meat.

iv.   Mix in the garlic, pepper, salt, c. of cheese, tomato paste, poblano, and onion. Stir until everything is well combined.

v.    Place the meat mixture in the peppers. Put the pan onto the grill, cover, and let them smoke for an hour.

vi.   Top the peppers with the remaining cheese and allow them to smoke, covered, for another 15 minutes. Serve.

**Servings| 4**                **Time required: Two hours**

# T-Bone with Blue Cheese Butter

## Ingredients:

- ❖ Two T. garlic, minced
- ❖ Two T. salt
- ❖ 4 One4- ounce T-bone steaks
- ❖ ½ c. crumbled blue cheese
- ❖ One T. pepper
- ❖ 4 T. room temperature butter

## Instructions:

i.   Mix the blue cheese and the butter together and set to the side. Do not refrigerate the butter unless you are making it way in advance.

ii.  Add wood pellets to your smoker and follow your cooker's startup procedure. Preheat your smoker, with your lid closed, until it reaches 165.

iii. Rub the steaks with the garlic, pepper, and salt.

iv.  Cover the steaks after putting them on. For about 30 mins., allow it to smoke.

v.   Turn the heat up to 450 and let the steaks smoke for 15 minutes if you like them medium-rare. Cook longer to reach your desired doneness.

vi.  Take the steaks off of the grill and let them rest for 3-5 minutes. Serve them topped with some of the blue cheese butter.

**Servings| 4**                    **Time required: One hour**

# Crispy Burnt Ends

## Ingredients:

- ❖ ¾ c. favorite barbecue sauce, divided
- ❖ 3 T. favorite dry rub
- ❖ 3 pounds chuck roast

## Instructions:

i.   Add wood pellets to your smoker and follow your cooker's startup procedure. Preheat your smoker, with your lid closed, until it reaches 275.

ii.  Liberally rub your chuck roast with your favorite dry rub.

iii. Lay the meat directly on the grill, cover, and allow it to smoke for around five minutes, or until it forms a dark bark on the surface and it reaches 165.

iv.  Use foil to wrap up the meat and continue to let it smoke, covered, for another hour or until it reaches 195.

v.   For about fifteen to twenty mins., let the roast rest after removing from the grill. Cut the roast into two-inch cubes.

vi.  Place the cubes on a disposable baking pan and toss them in a half c. barbecue sauce.

vii. Put the pan on the grill, cover, and allow it to smoke for another one hour and a half to two hours, or until they have become hot and bubbly. The remaining barbecue sauce could be added at the cooking's last thirty mins. Serve.

**Servings| 6**              **Time required: 8 hours**

# Roast Beast

## *Ingredients:*

- ❖ Two T. steak seasoning
- ❖ EVOO
- ❖ 3-4 pound rump roast
- ❖ One T. garlic, minced

## *Instructions:*

i.   Add wood pellets to your smoker and follow your cooker's startup procedure. Preheat your smoker, with your lid closed, until it reaches 425.

ii.  Rub the roast all over with a good amount of olive oil and then season with the steak seasoning and garlic.

iii. Lay the meat on the grill and then sear every side for about two to five minutes. Set it off of the grill.

iv.  Turn the heat of the smoker to 225.

v.   Lay the roast back on the grill, cover, and allow it to smoke for three to four hours. Depending on your desired doneness, it should reach a temperature of 120 to 155.

vi.  Use some foil to tent the roast after removing it from the heat. Allow the roast to rest for ten minutes and slice against the grain. Enjoy.

**Servings| 8-OneTwo**                    **Time required: 8-10 hours**

# Perfect Filet Mignon

## *Ingredients:*

- ❖ Two 1 ¼-inch thick filet mignons
- ❖ Two t. garlic, minced
- ❖ Two t. sea salt
- ❖ Two t. onion powder
- ❖ Two t. pepper

## *Instructions:*

i.   Add wood pellets to your smoker and follow your cooker's startup procedure. Preheat your smoker, with your lid closed, until it reaches 450.

ii.  Mix together the onion powder, garlic, pepper, and salt. Generously rub the mignons with the rub mixture.

iii. Place the steaks on the grill, cover, and allow them to smoke for seven minutes. Flip the steaks and allow them to cook for another five to seven minutes. Cook until the temperature reaches your desired doneness. The temperature will rise five degrees while resting, so make sure it comes five degrees under your desired degree.

iv.  Take them off the grill and let them rest for five minutes.

**Servings| Two**              **Time required: 25 minutes**

# Texas Shoulder Clod

## Ingredients:

- ❖ 13-15 pound shoulder clod
- ❖ One T. smoked paprika
- ❖ One T. garlic, minced
- ❖ ½ c. sea salt
- ❖ One T. cayenne
- ❖ One T. red pepper flakes
- ❖ ½ c. pepper

## Instructions:

i.   Mix together the paprika, cayenne, minced garlic, red pepper flakes, pepper, and salt. Rub the spice mixture into the shoulder.

ii.  Add wood pellets to your smoker and follow your cooker's startup procedure. Preheat your smoker, with your lid closed, until it reaches 250.

iii. Place the meat on your grill, cover, and allow the shoulder to smoke for 12 to 16 hours. It should reach a temperature of 195. Towards the end of the smoking time, you may want to wrap the shoulder with foil so that it doesn't burn.

iv.  Let the shoulder to rest for 15 minutes. Slice against the grain and serve.

**Servings| 16-20**                    **Time required: 16 hours**

# French Onion Burgers

## Ingredients:

- ❖ 4 slices provolone cheese
- ❖ One t. dried chives
- ❖ One loaf French bread, sliced into 8 slices
- ❖ 3 medium onions, thickly sliced
- ❖ ½ c. soy sauce
- ❖ One T. EVOO
- ❖ ½ c. soy sauce
- ❖ 8 slices gruyere cheese, divided
- ❖ One pound lean ground beef
- ❖ One T. garlic, minced
- ❖ One t. beef base
- ❖ One t. liquid smoke
- ❖ One t. pepper

## Instructions:

i. Combine the pepper, chives, beef base, garlic, and ground beef. Make sure that everything is well mixed. Divide the meat into eight burger patties. Top four patties with a slice of gruyere and place the other four patties on top. This will create four stuffed burgers.

ii. Add wood pellets to your smoker and follow your cooker's startup procedure. Preheat your smoker, with your lid closed, until it reaches 425.

iii. Cover the burgers after placing them on the grill. For ten mins., let it smoke. Cover the burgers again after flipping them on the other side. For another ten to fifteen minutes, cook them again. Lay another cheese slice on top of each burger during the last five minutes.

iv.     Meanwhile, mix together the liquid smoke, olive oil, and soy sauce. Place the onion slices on the grill and coat both sides with the soy sauce mixture. Allow the onions to smoke for 20 minutes, flipping at the halfway point.

v.      Toast the French bread slices on the grill. Place a patty on a bread slice, top with a slice of provolone, and then the smoked onions. Top with the second slice of bread. Serve.

**Servings| 4                    Time required: One hour**

# London Broil

## *Ingredients:*

- ❖ One t. pepper
- ❖ Two T. packed brown sugar
- ❖ Two minced garlic cloves
- ❖ ¼ c. soy sauce
- ❖ ¼ c. scallions, chopped
- ❖ Two T. EVOO
- ❖ Two t. red pepper flake
- ❖ Two T. white wine
- ❖ 1 ½ -2 pound London broil

## *Instructions:*

i. With a meat mallet, pound the steak lightly on both sides to tenderize the meat. You don't want to pound down the thickness, it's only for tenderizing.

ii. Mix the pepper, red pepper flakes, garlic, brown sugar, scallions, oil, wine, and soy sauce together to make the marinade. Lay the steak in a container and add in the marinade. Chill the covered meat for four hours.

iii. Take the steak out of the marinade and discard any remaining marinade.

iv. Add wood pellets to your smoker and follow your cooker's startup procedure. Preheat your smoker, with your lid closed, until it reaches 350.

v.    Lay the steak on the grate, cover, and smoke for six minutes. Flip the steak and smoke for 6-10 minutes more. Cooking time will depend on how well-done you want the steak to be.

vi.   Let the meat rest for ten minutes.

**Servings| 3-4**          **Time required: 5 hours**

# Brisket Grilled Cheese

## Ingredients:

- ❖ Two slices Texas toast
- ❖ One T. butter
- ❖ Two slices cheese
- ❖ 4-ounces leftover brisket

## Instructions:

i.   Add wood pellets to your smoker and follow your cooker's startup procedure. Preheat your smoker, with your lid closed, to high.

ii.  Lay a griddle on the grill. Butter the bread. Lay a slice of toast, buttered-side down, on the skillet. Place on a slice of cheese, brisket, and more cheese. Top with the second sliced of bread with the buttered side up.

iii. Cover, and smoke for five to seven minutes. Flip and smoke five more minutes.

iv.  Serve.

**Servings| One**                          **Time required: 15 minutes**

# Pork

## Sugar-Glazed Ham

### *Ingredients:*

- ❖ ½ t. cloves
- ❖ One t. cinnamon
- ❖ ¼ c. mustard
- ❖ ½ c. brown sugar
- ❖ One c. pineapple juice
- ❖ 12-15 pound bone-in cooked ham

### *Instructions:*

i. Add wood pellets to your smoker and follow your cooker's startup procedure. Preheat your smoker, with your lid closed, until it reaches 275.

ii. Trim the fat and skin from the ham. Place in a foil-lined roasting pan.

iii. Mix the other ingredients together in a pot and simmer for 15 minutes, or reduced by half.

iv. Baste the ham with the syrup mixture. Reserve some for later basting.

v. Lay on the grill, cover, and smoke for four hours. Baste the ham with the syrup mixture, cover, and smoke one more hour.

vi. Use a foil to tent the ham after removing from the grill. Before carving, let it rest for twenty minutes.

**Servings| 12-15**                **Time required: 5.5 hours**

# Country Pork Roast

## *Ingredients:*

- ❖ ¾ c. brown sugar
- ❖ 3 chopped apples
- ❖ 28-ounce jar sauerkraut
- ❖ Two pounds pork loin roast
- ❖ EVOO
- ❖ Two t. dried basil
- ❖ 3 T. Greek seasoning

## *Instructions:*

i. Add wood pellets to your smoker and follow your cooker's startup procedure. Preheat your smoker, with your lid closed, until it reaches 250.

ii. Mix the apples, sugar, and sauerkraut together. Spread this into a 9" x 13" casserole dish.

iii. Oil the roast and rub with the remaining seasonings. Place in the casserole dish and then sit on the grill and roast for three hours. It should reach 160.

iv. Take the roast out and let it rest for five minutes and slice. Serve with the apple mixture.

**Servings| 8**          **Time required: 3.5 hours**

# Scotch Eggs

## Ingredients:

- ❖ ¼ c. Dijon
- ❖ One c. mayonnaise
- ❖ One c. panko
- ❖ One beaten egg
- ❖ One pound hot sausage
- ❖ 4 peeled hard-boiled eggs
- ❖ 4 t. poultry seasoning, divided
- ❖ ½ c. all-purpose flour

## Instructions:

i.   Mix half of the poultry seasoning and the flour together. Wet the eggs in water and then roll in the flour mixture.

ii.  Split the sausage into four equal sections and form into balls. Flatten them and shape them around the eggs until covered.

iii. Beat the eggs and dip each sausage balls into them. In the panko, roll them next. Lay on a plate, cover, and chill for two hours.

iv.  Mix the remaining seasoning with the mustard and mayo. This will be the dipping sauce.

v.   Add wood pellets to your smoker and follow your cooker's startup procedure. Preheat your smoker, with your lid closed, on the smoke setting.

vi.  Place the eggs on the grill, cover, and smoke an hour. Remove them from the grill and turn the temperature to 375. Place the eggs back on, cover, and smoke 30 mins.

vii.    For approximately 5 mins, let them cool. Slice before serving with the sauce.

**Servings| 4-6**                 **Time required: 4 hours**

# Pulled Pork

## Ingredients:

- ❖ Barbecue sauce
- ❖ ½ c. salt
- ❖ Two c. apple juice
- ❖ ½ favorite rub, divided
- ❖ ¼ c. mustard
- ❖ 5 pound Boston butt

## Instructions:

i.   Rub the meat with the mustard and rub on ¼ c. of the dry rub. Mix the salt and apple juice in a spray bottle.

ii.  Add wood pellets to your smoker and follow your cooker's startup procedure. Preheat your smoker, with your lid closed, until it reaches 225.

iii. Lay the pork, fat-side up, on a pan and place on the grill. Cover and smoke 8-9 hours. Every hour, spritz with the juice mixture. It should reach 205. Tent with foil during the last few minutes of cooking if needed to prevent blackening.

iv.  Remove the liquid from the pan and then let the meat rest for a couple of minutes before shredding it. Coat with the sauce and rest of the tub.

v.   Serve.

**Servings| 10**            **Time required: 9.5 hours**

# Cream Cheese Sausage Balls

## Ingredients:

- ❖ One package mini filo-dough shells
- ❖ 8-ounces softened cream cheese
- ❖ One pound ground sausage

## Instructions:

i.    Add wood pellets to your smoker and follow your cooker's startup procedure. Preheat your smoker, with your lid closed, until it reaches 350.

ii.   Mix the cream cheese and sausage together. This is easier done with your hands than a spoon.

iii.  Lay the filo shells on a perforated pizza pan. Roll the sausage into balls and lay them in the shells. Grill, covered, and smoke 30 minutes.

iv.   Serve.

**Servings| 4-5**               **Time required: 45 minutes**

# Avocado Pork Chops

## Ingredients:

- ❖ Pepper
- ❖ Salt
- ❖ One t. garlic powder
- ❖ One c. avocado oil
- ❖ ½ t. garlic salt
- ❖ ½ t. onion powder
- ❖ Two pounds pork chops

## Instructions:

i. Put the pork chops into a large shallow container.

ii. In a mixing container, combine the avocado oil, garlic salt, garlic powder, onion powder, salt, and pepper. Combine the marinade and the pork chops before covering.

iii. In the fridge, place the marinade for a minimum of 4 hours. Overnight is also preferred.

iv. Add wood pellets to your smoker and follow your cooker's startup procedure. Preheat your smoker, with your lid closed, until it reaches 450.

v. Remove them from the container. Use paper towels to pat them dry. Place them onto the preheated grill and smoke for five minutes. Flip each one over and smoke five minutes more.

vi. Place the cooked pork chops onto a serving plate. Serve with salad and French fries.

**Servings| 6**                    **Time required: 4 hours 45 minutes**

# Pork Chops

## Ingredients:

- ❖ Pepper
- ❖ Salt
- ❖ Two cloves minced garlic
- ❖ Two T. tamari sauce
- ❖ One T. dry sherry
- ❖ 4 boneless pork chops
- ❖ ¼ c. honey
- ❖ ¼ c. lemon juice

## Instructions:

i. Put the pork chops into a zip top bag.

ii. Mix together the pepper, salt, garlic, tamari sauce, sherry, lemon juice, and honey.

iii. Pour this mixture over the pork chops.

iv. Refrigerate the chops overnight.

v. Add wood pellets to your smoker and follow your cooker's startup procedure. Preheat your smoker, with your lid closed, until it reaches 350.

vi. The pork chops should be taken out of the bag. Use paper towels to pat them dry. Reserve the marinade for later.

vii. On the grill that is already pre-heated, place the pork chops. For ten minutes, let them smoke. Flip each one over and cook for another 8 minutes.

viii.    While the pork chops are cooking the last eight minutes, add the marinade to a pot and allow it to come to a boil. Allow to simmer until the chops are cooked.

ix.    Lay pork chops onto a serving plate and pour marinade over top.

**Servings| 4**                   **Time required: 8 hours 55 minutes**

# Mandarin Pork Loin

## *Ingredients:*

- ❖ One c. mustard
- ❖ One t. white pepper
- ❖ One c. tangerine juice
- ❖ One T. garlic powder
- ❖ One c. honey
- ❖ 4 pounds pork loin
- ❖ Mandarin Habanero Seasoning Rub

## *Instructions:*

i.   Add wood pellets to your smoker and follow your cooker's startup procedure. Preheat your smoker, with the lid closed until it reaches 375.

ii.  Take the Mandarin Habanero Seasoning Rub and rub the pork loin generously all over.

iii. Add the pepper, garlic powder, tangerine juice, mustard, and honey in a pot. Stir well to combine. Let mixture come to a boil. Lower to a simmer.

iv.  Put the pork loin onto the hot grill, cover, and cook for 35 minutes.

v.   Once 15 minutes has passed, brush the pork loin with the sauce and continue to cook.

vi.  After it has cooked for 35 minutes, check the internal temperature. When it has reached 140 degrees, take it off the grill, wrap in foil, and let it rest for ten minutes.

vii. Slice and serve with more sauce f there is any left over.

**Servings| 8**                    **Time required: 1 hour 25 minutes**

# Pineapple Lemongrass Pork Chops

## Ingredients:

- ❖ ½ c. chopped cilantro
- ❖ ¼ c. pineapple juice
- ❖ ½ c. chicken broth
- ❖ Two T. minced garlic
- ❖ 4 T. lemongrass
- ❖ Two t. lime zest
- ❖ Two T. minced ginger
- ❖ 4 pork chops
- ❖ 3 T. fresh mint
- ❖ Lime wedges

## Instructions:

i. Mix together the lime zest, chicken broth, garlic, ginger, mint, cilantro, lemongrass, and pineapple juice.

ii. Place the pork chops into a large zip-top baggie and pour the marinade over.

iii. Seal and refrigerate overnight.

iv. Add wood pellets to your smoker and follow your cooker's startup procedure. Preheat your smoker, with your lid closed, until it reaches 450.

v. Take the pork chops out of the bag and drain. Throw away the leftover marinade. Place them onto the preheated grill and smoke for 4 minutes. Flip the pork chops on its other side. For another 3 mins., smoke them again.

vi.   Place the chops over indirect heat and cover. Cook until the internal temperature reaches about 145.

**Servings| 4**                    **Time required: 8 hours 45 minutes**

# Lavender Thyme Pork Chops

## Ingredients:

- ❖ Pepper
- ❖ Salt
- ❖ Two T. olive oil
- ❖ Two cloves minced garlic
- ❖ ¼ c. honey
- ❖ 3 t. dried cooking lavender
- ❖ Two t. chopped thyme
- ❖ Two t. brown sugar
- ❖ Two t. balsamic vinegar
- ❖ 4 pork chops
- ❖ 4 ripe plums

## Instructions:

i.   Put the pork chops into a bag.

ii.  Mix together the pepper, salt, garlic, thyme, brown sugar, lavender, and olive oil.

iii. Pour this mixture over the pork chops. Allow to set on the counter for 30 minutes.

iv.  While pork chops are marinating, heat the balsamic vinegar and honey in a pot. Constantly stir until ingredients have thoroughly combined. Set this to the side.

v.   Add wood pellets to your smoker and follow your cooker's startup procedure. Preheat your smoker, with your lid closed, until it reaches 225.

vi.     The pork chops should be removed from the bag before patting them dry using the paper towels. Let them smoke for about 5 mins., after placing them on the grill that was pre-heated. Flip them over and smoke for four more minutes. Continue to cook until internal temperature reaches 140.

vii.    Slice the plums in half and take out the pit. Lay them cut side down on the grill until golden or for a couple of minutes.

viii.   Brush the plums with a honey glaze on both sides and cook another minute.

ix.     Top the pork chops with the sauce and serve with the plums.

**Servings| 4**                    **Time required: 1 hour 5 minutes**

# Citrusy Herbed Pork Cutlets

## Ingredients:

- ❖ Pepper
- ❖ Salt
- ❖ Two T. olive oil
- ❖ Juice of one orange
- ❖ One t. ground caraway
- ❖ Two T. chopped parsley
- ❖ 10 twigs of cilantro
- ❖ One clove minced garlic
- ❖ 4 pork cutlets
- ❖ Juice of two lemons

## Instructions:

i. Put the pork cutlets into a zip top bag.

ii. Mix together the pepper, salt, olive oil, garlic, caraway, parsley, cilantro, orange juice, and lemon juice.

iii. Pour this mixture over the pork.

iv. Place into the refrigerator for four hours.

v. Add wood pellets to your smoker and follow your cooker's startup procedure. Preheat your smoker, with your lid closed, until it reaches 450.

vi. Remove the pork cutlets from the bag. Use paper towels to pat them dry. Place them onto the preheated grill and smoke for ten minutes. Flip over the pork and smoke ten minutes more.

**Servings| 4**                    **Time required: 4 hours 45 minutes**

# Anise Honey Beer Pork Loin

## Ingredients:

- ❖ Pepper
- ❖ Salt
- ❖ One T. chopped thyme
- ❖ 3 T. mustard
- ❖ One t. anise seed
- ❖ One c. dark beer
- ❖ ¼ c. honey
- ❖ One diced red onion
- ❖ 3 pounds pork loin

## Instructions:

i.   Put the pork loin in a bag.

ii.  Mix together the pepper, salt, thyme, mustard, beer, anise, red onion, and honey.

iii. Pour this mixture over the pork loin. Seal the bag and place in the refrigerator for four hours.

iv.  Add wood pellets to your smoker and follow your cooker's startup procedure. Preheat your smoker, with your lid closed, until it reaches 350.

v.   When ready to grill, take the pork out of the bag and place on a paper towel. Take the marinade and pour it into a saucepan.

vi.  Place pork loin onto the grill and cook for one hour with the lid up. Boil the marinade for five minutes and as the pork cooks, take the marinade and brush the pork loin generously. Continue to cook for another 45 minutes.

vii.   Pork is done when the internal temperature reaches 165. Take off from the grill and let it rest for ten minutes before serving.

**Servings| 6**                    **Time required: 7 hours 20 minutes**

# Hot Paprika Pork Tenderloin

## Ingredients:

- ❖ Pepper
- ❖ Salt
- ❖ One T. oregano
- ❖ Two T. hot paprika
- ❖ ½ c. tomato basil sauce
- ❖ ¾ c. chicken broth
- ❖ Two pounds pork tenderloin

## Instructions:

i. In a bowl, put the pepper, salt, oregano, paprika, tomato basil sauce, and chicken stock. Stir well to combine.

ii. Brush the pork tenderloin generously with mixture.

iii. Add wood pellets to your smoker and follow your cooker's startup procedure. Preheat your smoker, with your lid closed, until it reaches 225.

iv. Place the pork onto the grill and smoke for three hours or until it reaches 145.

v. After removing from the grill, use the foil to cover them. Before slicing, let them cool for approximately 10 mins.

**Servings| 6**               **Time required: 3 hours 35 minutes**

# Herbed Pork Rib Roast

## Ingredients:

- ❖ Pepper
- ❖ Salt
- ❖ ¼ c. olive oil
- ❖ One T. crushed fennel seeds
- ❖ One t. chopped parsley
- ❖ One T. minced garlic
- ❖ One t. chopped rosemary
- ❖ One t. chopped sage
- ❖ 3 pounds bone-in pork rib roast

## Instructions:

i. In a bowl, put the pepper, salt, rosemary, sage, parsley, fennel, garlic, and olive oil. Stir well to combine.

ii. Coat the rib roast generously with the herbs.

iii. Add wood pellets to your smoker and follow your cooker's startup procedure. Preheat your smoker, with your lid closed, until it reaches 350.

iv. Place the roast onto the grill and smoke for three hours.

v. Take off the grill, cover, and let it rest for ten minutes. Slice between each rib to make a pork chop and place them on a serving platter.

**Servings|6**          **Time required: 3 hours 20 minutes**

# Mexican Pineapple Pork Tenderloin

## Ingredients:

For Pork:

- ❖ Two T. lime juice
- ❖ Two pounds pork tenderloin
- ❖ ¼ t. cayenne pepper
- ❖ ½ t. pepper
- ❖ One t. ground cumin

For Marinade:

- ❖ ¼ t. cayenne pepper
- ❖ ¼ c. orange juice
- ❖ Two T. Worcestershire sauce
- ❖ ¼ c. lime juice
- ❖ One 11 oz can unsweetened crushed pineapple
- ❖ One 11 oz can roasted tomatoes
- ❖ ½ c. port wine
- ❖ One t. garlic powder
- ❖ ¼ c. brown sugar

## Instructions:

i.  Put the lime juice, cayenne, pepper, and cumin and rub generously on the tenderloin.

ii. Add wood pellets to your smoker and follow your cooker's startup procedure. Preheat your smoker, with your lid closed, until it reaches 225.

iii.  Place the tenderloin onto the grill and smoke it for three hours or until it reaches 145. Take off the grill and let sit for five minutes before you slice it.

For Sauce:

i.  The sauce ingredients should be placed in a saucepan before boiling. For about twenty mins., simmer the sauce until it is almost half the original amount. Stir the mixture occasionally. Take off heat and let cool for a little while.

ii.  Slice the tenderloin and serve with sauce.

**Servings| 6**                      **ime required: 3 hours 55 minutes**

# Candied Spareribs

## Ingredients:

- ❖ One c. barbecue sauce
- ❖ ¼ c. apple juice, divided
- ❖ Two T. mustard
- ❖ One T. red pepper flakes
- ❖ Two T. chicken bouillon granules
- ❖ Two racks pork spareribs, membrane removed

## Instructions:

i. Add wood pellets to your smoker and follow your cooker's startup procedure. Preheat your smoker, with your lid closed, until it reaches 250.

ii. Rub the ribs with mustard and then coat with the pepper flakes and bouillon.

iii. Place them on the grill, cover, and smoke for three hours.

iv. Remove from the grill and wrap the wraps with foil. Before sealing tightly, add in Two T. of juice to each pack.

v. Place them on the grill, cover, and smoke for two hours.

vi. Carefully unwrap and baste with the barbecue sauce. Cover and cook for another hour.

vii. Let them rest for five minutes and serve with extra sauce.

**Servings| 4-5**              **Time required: 6 hours**

# Smoked Sausage

## Ingredients:

- ❖ Ketchup
- ❖ Dijon
- ❖ 8 buns
- ❖ One t. chopped basil
- ❖ 8 Italian sausages

## Instructions:

i.   Add wood pellets to your smoker and follow your cooker's startup procedure. Preheat your smoker, with your lid closed, until it reaches 250.

ii.  Lay the sausage on the grill, cover, and smoke for 30-35 minutes. Turn the heat to 325 to brown up the outside.

iii. Place on a plate and serve on a bun with ketchup and mustard.

**Servings| 8**              **Time required: 50 minutes**

# Spicy Sausages

## Ingredients:

- ❖ Two pounds spicy sausages
- ❖ Pepper
- ❖ One T. chopped capers
- ❖ One c. yogurt
- ❖ 3 T. wine vinegar
- ❖ 1/3 c. Dijon

## Instructions:

i. Prick the sausages with a fork.

ii. Add wood pellets to your smoker and follow your cooker's startup procedure. Preheat your smoker, with your lid closed, until it reaches 250.

iii. Place on the grills, cover, and cook for 10-12 minutes on both sides.

iv. The remaining ingredients should be combined together before serving with sausage.

**Servings| 6**          **Time required: 20 minutes**

# Sausage with Sherry Peppers

## Ingredients:

- ❖ Two t. sherry vinegar
- ❖ 3 bell peppers
- ❖ 16 - Ounces smoked sausage
- ❖ ¼ t. kosher salt
- ❖ Two T. honey

## Instructions:

i.   Add wood pellets to your smoker and follow your cooker's startup procedure. Preheat your smoker, with your lid closed, until it reaches 350.

ii.  Mix the salt, honey, and sherry together.

iii. Slice the sausages lengthwise. Place the peppers and sausages on the grill, cover, and cook for four minutes on both sides.

iv.  Take the charred skin off the peppers and slice into strips. Slice sausage into 4-inch pieces. Toss the peppers in the sauce and serve with the sausage.

**Servings| 4**                    **Time required: 10 minutes**

# Poultry

## Ranch Wings

### Ingredients:

- ❖ Two pounds chicken wings
- ❖ Two T. EVOO
- ❖ Two packages ranch dressing mix

### Instructions:

i.   Add wood pellets to your smoker and follow your cooker's startup procedure. Preheat your smoker, with your lid closed, until it reaches 350.

ii.  Toss the wings in oil and ranch dressing mix. Place them on the grill, close the lid, and smoke for 25 minutes. Flip, and smoke for another 20-35 minutes. They should reach 165.

iii. Serve them with ranch dressing if desired.

**Servings| 4**               **Time required: One hour**

# Barbecue Chicken

## Ingredients:

- ❖ 8 Chicken breasts
- ❖ Two t. salt
- ❖ Two c. barbecue sauce, divided
- ❖ Two t. garlic powder
- ❖ Two t. pepper

## Instructions:

i. Add wood pellets to your smoker and follow your cooker's startup procedure. Preheat your smoker, with your lid closed, until it reaches 250.

ii. Rub the chicken with the spices and lay in a roasting pan. Cover the chicken before placing them on the grill. For about two hours, let them smoke. It should reach 165. During the last 15 minutes, baste with a c. of barbecue sauce.

iii. Serve with the rest of the sauce.

**Servings| 8**          **Time required: Two hours**

# Whole Turkey

## Ingredients:

- ❖ Two t. thyme
- ❖ Two t. sage
- ❖ ½ c. apple juice
- ❖ One stick melted butter
- ❖ ¼ c. poultry seasoning
- ❖ EVOO
- ❖ 10-12 pound turkey

## Instructions:

i.   Add wood pellets to your smoker and follow your cooker's startup procedure. Preheat your smoker, with your lid closed, until it reaches 250.

ii.  Rub the oil and seasoning on the turkey. Get some in under the skin as well as inside.

iii. Mix the thyme, sage, juice, and butter together.

iv.  Place the turkey in a roasting pan, put it on the grill, cover, and cook 5-6 hours. Baste it every hour with the juice mixture. It should reach 165. Let it rest for 15-20 minutes before carving.

**Servings| 8-6**          **Time required: 6 hours**

# Barbecue Chicken Breasts

## Ingredients:

- ❖ Two T. Worcestershire sauce
- ❖ ½ c. hot barbecue sauce
- ❖ One c. barbecue sauce
- ❖ Two cloves minced garlic
- ❖ ¼ c. olive oil
- ❖ 4 chicken breasts

## Instructions:

i.   Put the chicken breasts into a deep container.

ii.  In another bowl, put the Worcestershire sauce, barbecue sauces, garlic, and olive oil. Stir well to combine.

iii. Use half to marinate the chicken and reserve the rest for basting.

iv.  Add wood pellets to your smoker and follow your cooker's startup procedure. Preheat your smoker, with your lid closed, until it reaches 350.

v.   Take the chicken breasts out of the sauce. On the grill, place them before smoking them for approximately 20 minutes.

vi.  About ten minutes before the chicken is finished, baste with reserved barbecue sauce.

**Servings| 4**              **Time required: 45 minutes**

# Cilantro-Lime Chicken

## Ingredients:

- ❖ Pepper
- ❖ Salt
- ❖ 4 cloves minced garlic
- ❖ ½ c. lime juice
- ❖ One c. honey
- ❖ Two T. olive oil
- ❖ ½ c. chopped cilantro
- ❖ 4 chicken breasts

## Instructions:

i.    Put the chicken breasts into a large zip-top bag.

ii.   In another bowl, put the pepper, salt, olive oil, garlic, honey, lime juice, and cilantro. Stir well to combine.

iii.  Use half as a marinade and reserve the rest for later.

iv.   Place into the refrigerator for four to five hours.

v.    Add wood pellets to your smoker and follow your cooker's startup procedure. Preheat your smoker, with your lid closed, until it reaches 350.

vi.   Remove the chicken breasts the bag. Use paper towels to pat them dry. Let them smoke up in the grill for about fifteen mins.

vii.  About five minutes before the chicken is finished, baste with reserved marinade.

**Servings| 4**              **Time required: 5 hours**

# Lemon Honey Chicken

## Ingredients:

- ❖ Pepper
- ❖ Salt
- ❖ Chopped rosemary
- ❖ One clove crushed garlic
- ❖ One T. honey
- ❖ Juice of one lemon
- ❖ ½ c. chicken broth
- ❖ 3 T. butter
- ❖ 4 chicken breasts

## Instructions:

i.   Place a pan on the stove and melt the butter. Place chicken breasts into hot butter and sear on each side until a nice color has formed.

ii.  Take out of the pan and allow to rest for ten minutes.

iii. In a small bowl, put the pepper, salt, rosemary, garlic, honey, lemon juice, and broth. Stir well to combine.

iv.  Rub each breast with the honey lemon mixture.

v.   Add wood pellets to your smoker and follow your cooker's startup procedure. Preheat your smoker, with your lid closed, until it reaches 350.

vi.  Put the chicken breasts onto the preheated grill and grill for 20 minutes.

**Servings| 4**               **Time required: 55 minutes**

# Herbed Coffee Chicken

## *Ingredients:*

- ❖ Salt
- ❖ ¾ c. strong brewed coffee
- ❖ One t. coriander seeds
- ❖ 4 lemon slices
- ❖ One t. peppercorns
- ❖ One t. mustard seeds
- ❖ ½ c. chicken broth
- ❖ ¼ c. dark brown sugar, packed
- ❖ Two T. melted butter
- ❖ 4 chicken breast halves

## *Instructions:*

i.   Rub the butter on the chicken and rub in the salt.

ii.  In a large container, stir together the remaining ingredients. Cover the chicken with marinade.

iii. Place into the refrigerator for two hours.

iv.  Add wood pellets to your smoker and follow your cooker's startup procedure. Preheat your smoker, with your lid closed, until it reaches 350.

v.   Smoke the chicken for ten minutes. There's no need to flip. Serve.

**Servings| 4**                    **Time required: 2hours 40 minutes**

# Red Pepper Chicken Thighs

## Ingredients:

- ❖ One T. garlic powder
- ❖ One t. curry powder
- ❖ One t. red pepper flakes
- ❖ One t. black pepper
- ❖ Two T. olive oil
- ❖ ½ c. chicken broth
- ❖ One t. oregano
- ❖ One t. paprika
- ❖ Two pounds chicken thighs

## Instructions:

i.   Put the chicken thighs into a large flat dish in a single layer.

ii.  In a bowl, put the olive oil, garlic powder, curry, oregano, pepper, paprika, red pepper flakes, and broth. Stir well to combine.

iii. The mixture should be poured on top of the chicken.

iv.  Let the chicken marinate for four hours.

v.   Add wood pellets to your smoker and follow your cooker's startup procedure. Preheat your smoker, with your lid closed, until it reaches 450.

vi.  The chicken thighs should be removed from the bag. Use paper towels to pat them dry. Place them onto the preheated grill with the skin down and smoke for ten minutes. Turnover and cook for an additional ten minutes.

**Servings| 6**                    **Time required: 4 hours 45 minutes**

# Spicy Chicken Thighs

## *Ingredients:*

- ❖ One T. dry barbecue spice
- ❖ One t. coriander
- ❖ One T. oregano
- ❖ 1/3 c. balsamic vinegar
- ❖ Salt
- ❖ Two T. mustard
- ❖ 1/3 c. olive oil
- ❖ Pepper
- ❖ Two cloves minced garlic
- ❖ 6 chicken thighs

## *Instructions:*

i. Put the chicken thighs into a shallow dish in one layer.

ii. In a bowl, put the dry barbecue spice, coriander, oregano, pepper, salt, mustard, olive oil, balsamic vinegar, and garlic. Stir well to combine.

iii. Use the mixture to coat the chicken.

iv. Place into the refrigerator for four hours.

v. Add wood pellets to your smoker and follow your cooker's startup procedure. Preheat your smoker, with your lid closed, until it reaches 350.

vi. Remove the thighs of the chicken from the dish and use paper towels to pat them dry. Place them onto the preheated grill with the skin down and smoke for ten minutes. Flip them and cook an additional ten minutes.

**Servings| 6**                    **Time required: 4 hours 45 minutes**

# Turkey Burgers

## Ingredients:

- ❖ ½ t. oregano
- ❖ ½ t. thyme
- ❖ Pepper
- ❖ Salt
- ❖ One large egg
- ❖ ½ bunch chopped parsley
- ❖ Two pounds ground turkey
- ❖ One small chopped red bell pepper
- ❖ One finely chopped onion

## Instructions:

i.   Put all ingredients into a large bowl.

ii.  Use your hands and mix all ingredients until combined well.

iii. Make six patties. You can dip your hands into the water if the meat begins sticking to your hands.

iv.  Add wood pellets to your smoker and follow your cooker's startup procedure. Preheat your smoker, with your lid closed, until it reaches 350.

v.   Place them on the grill and smoke for five minutes, covered, until grill marks form. Turn each burger over and cook for an additional five minutes.

vi.  Check to see if the internal temperature of the burgers has reached 165.

vii. Serve with favorite burger toppings.

**Servings| 6**                    **Time required: 40 minutes**

# Turmeric Chicken

## Ingredients:

- ❖ Salt
- ❖ One t. turmeric
- ❖ ½ c. bacon fat
- ❖ 4 cloves minced garlic
- ❖ 4 chicken breasts

## Instructions:

i. Put the chicken breasts into a large shallow dish.

ii. In another bowl, put the garlic, turmeric, bacon fat, and salt. Stir well to combine.

iii. Rub each chicken breast generously with the mixture.

iv. Add wood pellets to your smoker and follow your cooker's startup procedure. Preheat your smoker, with your lid closed, until it reaches 350.

v. For about 10 mins., smoke the chicken on the grill. Flip them and smoke for ten minutes more.

**Servings| 4**          **Time required: 45 minutes**

# Mediterranean Chicken

## Ingredients:

- ❖ Lemon slices to garnish
- ❖ Salt
- ❖ Pepper
- ❖ One t. chopped rosemary
- ❖ 3 cloves minced garlic
- ❖ Zest of one lemon
- ❖ One t. oregano
- ❖ small chopped onion
- ❖ ½ c. white wine
- ❖ ¼ c. olive oil
- ❖ 4 chicken breasts

## Instructions:

i.   Put the chicken breasts into a large zip-top bag.

ii.  In another bowl, put the olive oil, white wine, lemon zest, onion, garlic, oregano, rosemary, pepper, and salt. Stir well to combine.

iii. Coat the chicken in this mixture.

iv.  Place into the refrigerator for two to three hours.

v.   Add wood pellets to your smoker and follow your cooker's startup procedure. Preheat your smoker, with your lid closed, until it reaches 350.

vi.  The chicken breast should be removed from the bag before patting them dry with paper towels. Place them on the grill and smoke for 15 minutes.

vii. Let it rest for 10 minutes before slicing. Garnish with sliced lemon.

**Servings| 6   Time required: 3 hours 6 minutes**

# Pineapple Turkey Wings

## Ingredients:

- ❖ Pepper
- ❖ Salt
- ❖ ¼ t. garlic powder
- ❖ Two pounds turkey wings
- ❖ One T. packed brown sugar
- ❖ Two t. chili powder
- ❖ One 11-ounce can pineapple, undrained
- ❖ ¼ t. ground ginger
- ❖ One 11-ounce can tomato sauce

## Instructions:

i.   Put the turkey wings into a large dish. Make sure they are in one layer.

ii.  In a bowl, put the pepper, salt, garlic powder, ginger, chili powder, brown sugar, pineapple, and tomato sauce. Combine thoroughly.

iii. This mixture should be poured on the turkey.

iv.  Place into the refrigerator for four to five hours.

v.   Add wood pellets to your smoker and follow your cooker's startup procedure. Preheat your smoker, with your lid closed, until it reaches 350.

vi.  Take the turkey wings out of the marinade. Use the paper towels to pat them dry. Place them onto the grill and smoke for 5 minutes on both sides. Move to cool side and allow to smoke for an additional 40 minutes.

vii. Internal temperature needs to be 165.

**Servings| 6**          **Time required: 6 hours 15 minutes**

# Cheesy Turkey Patties

## *Ingredients:*

- ❖ Pepper
- ❖ One t. chili powder
- ❖ Two wheat pita rounds, cut in half
- ❖ ½ avocado
- ❖ ¼ c. light cream cheese
- ❖ One tomato
- ❖ ¼ c. shredded cheddar
- ❖ One cucumber
- ❖ Two t. chopped green onion
- ❖ One t. oregano
- ❖ One pound ground turkey
- ❖ Salt

## *Instructions:*

i.   Place the oregano, pepper, salt, and turkey into a bowl.

ii.  Mix everything together with your hands. Form into four patties.

iii. Add wood pellets to your smoker and follow your cooker's startup procedure. Preheat your smoker, with your lid closed, until it reaches 380.

iv.  Smoke the patties on the grill. Each side should take approximately five mins.

v.   While patties are cooking, mix together the cheddar cheese, cream cheese, chili powder, green onion, and salt.

vi.     Slice the pita bread open and spread the mixture onto the inside of the pita. Place a turkey patty inside along with cucumber, tomato, and avocado slices.

**Servings| 4   Time required: 25 minutes**

# Chicken Patties

## Ingredients:

- ❖ Pepper
- ❖ Salt
- ❖ Two t. paprika
- ❖ 2/3 c. minced onion
- ❖ Two T. chopped parsley
- ❖ Two T. lemon juice
- ❖ One T. chopped cilantro
- ❖ Pinch red pepper flakes
- ❖ ½ t. cumin
- ❖ Two T. olive oil
- ❖ Two pounds ground chicken

## Instructions:

i.   Wash and finely chop the onions. Mix the onions with the rest of the ingredients

ii.  Use your hands and combine all the ingredients. Keep mixing until you have thoroughly mixed all the ingredients together. Form into six patties. Refrigerate them for 20 minutes

iii. Add wood pellets to your smoker and follow your cooker's startup procedure. Preheat your smoker, with your lid closed, until it reaches 350.

iv.  Smoke each side of the patties on the grill for about ten mins.

v.   Serve on buns with toppings of your choice.

**Servings| 6**                    **Time required: 45 minutes**

# Parmesan Wings

## Ingredients:

- ❖ 3 T. parsley One c. parmesan
- ❖ ½ c. + Two T. favorite rub
- ❖ One0 diced garlic cloves
- ❖ One c. butter
- ❖ 5 pounds chicken wings

## Instructions:

i. Add wood pellets to your smoker and follow your cooker's startup procedure. Preheat your smoker, with your lid closed, to high.

ii. Toss wings in ½ c. of rub. Lay them on the grill, cover, and smoke for 10 minutes. Flip and smoke for 10 more minutes.

iii. Cook the remaining rub, butter, and garlic in a pot for 8-10 minutes.

iv. Toss the cook wings in the butter mixture and parmesan and parsley.

v. Serve.

**Servings| 4-6**          **Time required: 40 minutes**

# Jerk Chicken

## *Ingredients:*

- ❖ One T. whole allspice
- ❖ ½ c. jerk paste
- ❖ ¼ c. canola oil
- ❖ 4 chicken leg quarters, scored

## *Instructions:*

i.   Add wood pellets to your smoker and follow your cooker's startup procedure. Preheat your smoker, with your lid closed, until it reaches 275.

ii.  Brush the chicken with oil and the jerk paste. Reserve Two T. of paste.

iii. Place the allspice in with the wood pellets.

iv.  Lay the chicken on the grill, cover, and smoke for up to an hour and a half. It should reach 165.

v.   Let the chicken rest for five minutes and baste with the jerk paste before serving.

**Servings| 4**                    **Time required: Two hours**

# Seafood

## Ingredients:

- ❖ Smoked Pesto Mussels
- ❖ One c. white wine
- ❖ Two T. pine nuts
- ❖ One T. minced garlic
- ❖ One c. water
- ❖ ¼ c. basil
- ❖ ½ c. parmesan
- ❖ ¾ c. EVOO, divided
- ❖ Two pounds cleaned mussels

## Instructions:

i.   Boil the water and wine and add in a layer of mussels. Steam for 1-2 minutes. Discard the ones that aren't open. Continue until all of the mussels have been steamed. Strain the liquid and place to the side.

ii.  Remove the meat of the mussels and add into the liquid. Soak for 20 minutes.

iii. In a food processor, mix the remaining ingredients with ½ c. oil. Refrigerate pesto until needed.

iv.  Place the wood pellets to your smoker and follow your cooker's startup procedure. Preheat your smoker, with your lid closed, until it reaches 150.

v.   Put the mussels in a grill basket, cover, and smoke an hour and a half.

vi.  Toss the mussels in the pest and serve.

**Servings| Two-3**                    **Time required: Two hours**

# Tuna Steaks

## *Ingredients:*

- ❖ 4 6-8-ounce tuna steaks
- ❖ One t. pepper
- ❖ One t. ginger
- ❖ ¼ c. chopped scallions
- ❖ One lemon, juiced
- ❖ One T. minced garlic
- ❖ 1 ½ c. soy sauce t. onion powder
- ❖ Two T. sesame oil

## *Instructions:*

i.   Mix the scallions, ginger, pepper, onion powder, garlic, lemon juice, soy sauce, and sesame oil together. Cover the steaks with the marinade and refrigerate for an hour.

ii.  Add wood pellets to your smoker and follow your cooker's startup procedure. Preheat your smoker, with your lid closed, until it reaches 250.

iii. Place the steaks on the grill, cover, and smoke an hour. It should reach between 125 and 145.

iv.  Serve.

**Servings| 4**                         **Time required: Two hours**

# Herbed Mustard Calamari

## Ingredients:

- ❖ Pepper
- ❖ ½ bunch chopped parsley
- ❖ 4 t. sweet mustard
- ❖ Juice of two lemons
- ❖ Two T. chopped oregano
- ❖ Two c. milk
- ❖ 8 calamari, cleaned

## Instructions:

i. Thoroughly clean the calamari and slice evenly.

ii. In a metal dish, place the calamari before pouring the milk. Refrigerate overnight.

iii. Take the calamari out of the milk and drain well the next day. Pat them dry.

iv. Lightly oil the fish with the olive oil.

v. Place the lemon juice and mustard into a bowl. Whisk constantly as you pour in the olive oil slowly. Continue to whisk until everything is well-combined.

vi. Add in the pepper and oregano and stir again until combined.

vii. Add wood pellets to your smoker and follow your cooker's startup procedure. Preheat your smoker, with your lid closed, until it reaches 350.

viii.     For two minutes per side, smoke the calamari in the grill. They should be charred a bit. Take off the grill. Use a serving platter to serve.

ix.     Drizzle parsley and sauce on the top.

**Servings| 6**            **Time required: 35 minutes**

# Grilled Cuttlefish

## *Ingredients:*

- ❖ Salt
- ❖ ½ c. olive oil
- ❖ 8 large cuttlefish, cleaned
- ❖ One t. oregano
- ❖ ½ c. chopped cilantro
- ❖ One T. lemon juice

## *Instructions:*

i.   Make the marinade by mixing the salt, oregano, lemon juice, and olive. Don't add too much salt.

ii.  After placing the fish on the marinade, toss them so that they are coated evenly.

iii. Let it rest for an hour.

iv.  Take the fish out of the marinade and pat dry.

v.   Add wood pellets to your smoker and follow your cooker's startup procedure. Preheat your smoker, with your lid closed, until it reaches 450.

vi.  Place the fish onto the grill and smoke for 3 minutes on both sides. Serve.

**Servings| 6**            **Time required: 1 hour 30 minutes**

# Dijon Lemon Catfish

## Ingredients:

- ❖ Salt  ½ c. olive oil
- ❖ One t. paprika
- ❖ Two T. Dijon mustard
- ❖ Juice of four lemons
- ❖ One T. chopped rosemary
- ❖ 4 8 oz catfish fillets
- ❖ Pepper

## Instructions:

i.   Add wood pellets to your smoker and follow your cooker's startup procedure. Preheat your smoker, with your lid closed, until it reaches 350.

ii.  In a bowl, put the rosemary, paprika, salt, mustard, lemon juice, and olive oil. Stir well to combine.

iii. Brush one side of each fillet with the mixture. Season with pepper and salt.

iv.  The side of the fillets that has been season should be placed down on the grill. Cover them before cooking for about five mins. While this side is cooking, brush the fillets with the olive oil mixture. Turn fillets over and if you have any olive oil mixture left, brush some more over fillets. Cook for another five minutes on the second side.

v.   Remove from the grill and place on serving platter sprinkle with rosemary.

**Servings| 6**                    **Time required: 20 minutes**

# Chili Rosemary Halibut

## Ingredients:

- ❖ One rosemary twig
- ❖ One c. EVOO
- ❖ One bay leaf
- ❖ Two chopped red chili peppers
- ❖ Two cloves garlic
- ❖ Two lemons
- ❖ 4 T. white vinegar
- ❖ 4 halibut fillets

## Instructions:

i.   Place the white vinegar, lemon juice, rosemary, bay leaf, garlic, red chili, and olive oil into a large container. Mix well to combine.

ii.  Add in halibut fillets and toss to coat.

iii. Refrigerate for four hours.

iv.  Take halibut fillets out of the marinade and dry.

v.   Add wood pellets to your smoker and follow your cooker's startup procedure. Preheat your smoker, with your lid closed, until it reaches 350.

vi.  Place the halibut fillets on the grill and smoke for ten minutes. The flesh should be opaque.

vii. Turn only once so the halibut doesn't fall apart.

viii. Transfer to a serving platter, sprinkle on some rosemary, pour on some lemon juice, and serve.

**Servings| 6                    Time required: 4 hours 55 minutes**

# Lemon Butter Parsley Lobster

## *Ingredients:*

- ❖ Pepper
- ❖ Salt
- ❖ Two T. parsley
- ❖ Juice of two lemons
- ❖ ½ c. butter
- ❖ 4 lobsters

## *Instructions:*

i.   Find a pot that is big enough for all the lobsters to fit into. Fill with water and salt it. Boil the water before adding in the lobster. Boil for five minutes.

ii.   Remove the lobsters to a work surface.

iii.   Take hold of the lobster at the base of the head and cut the head off. Hold the body firmly and turn the abdomen toward you. Using a shape knife, cut up the middle of the lobster.

iv.   Add wood pellets to your smoker and follow your cooker's startup procedure. Preheat your smoker, with your lid closed, until it reaches 350.

v.   Melt the butter; add pepper, salt, parsley, and lemon juice. Mix well to combine. Spread some butter over the lobster. They should be put in the grill.

vi.   Grill lobster cut side down about eight minutes. Turn lobster over and brush on more butter. Grill for an additional five minutes.

vii.   Serve hot sprinkled with parsley and lemon butter.

**Servings| 4**            **Time required: 40 minutes**

# French Antilles Salmon Skewers

## Ingredients:

- ❖ Pepper
- ❖ Salt
- ❖ ¼ t. cayenne pepper
- ❖ 5 chopped green onions
- ❖ 3 tomatoes, cubed
- ❖ 3 cloves minced garlic
- ❖ Two pounds fresh salmon
- ❖ Zest of one lime
- ❖ Juice of one lime
- ❖ One c. chopped cilantro
- ❖ ½ c. olive oil

## Instructions:

i. Mix the lime zest, lime juice, half the cilantro, and oil in a deep dish.

ii. Cut the salmon into thick cubes and place into the marinade. Chill for 30 minutes.

iii. Mix the remaining ingredients to make the French Antilles sauce.

iv. Add wood pellets to your smoker and follow your cooker's startup procedure. Preheat your smoker, with your lid closed, until it reaches 350.

v. Place the salmon onto the skewers. Place on the grill for 12 minutes and cook on all sides.

vi. Serve with the French Antilles sauce and enjoy

**Servings| 8**                    **Time required: One hour**

# Cilantro Buttered Salmon

## Ingredients:

- ❖ Two T. lime juice
- ❖ One t. coriander
- ❖ ½ t. red pepper flakes
- ❖ ½ t. sea salt
- ❖ One t. minced garlic
- ❖ ¼ c. chopped cilantro
- ❖ ½ c. softened butter
- ❖ 4 6 oz. skin on salmon fillets

## Instructions:

i.   Put the red pepper flakes, salt, coriander, lime juice, garlic, cilantro, and butter into a mixing container. Combine them well by mixing them together.

ii.  Brush the salmon fillets generously with the mixture. Let this sit at room temp for 15 minutes.

iii. Add wood pellets to your smoker and follow your cooker's startup procedure. Preheat your smoker, with your lid closed, until it reaches 350.

iv.  Place on the grill skin side down, uncovered, don't touch for ten minutes. Gently turn over and cook an additional ten minutes.

**Servings| 6**                    **Time required: 1 hour 36 minutes**

# Crab Legs

## *Ingredients:*

- ❖ One T. Cajun seasoning
- ❖ Two T. lemon juice
- ❖ One c. melted butter
- ❖ Two cloves minced garlic
- ❖ 3 pounds crab legs
- ❖ Lemon wedges

## *Instructions:*

i. Place the crab legs into a large roasting pan.

ii. Put the garlic, butter, and lemon juice into a bowl and whisk together. Pour this mixture over the crab legs. Sprinkle with Cajun seasoning.

iii. Add wood pellets to your smoker and follow your cooker's startup procedure. Preheat your smoker, with your lid closed, until it reaches 350.

iv. Place the roasting pan into the smoker. Take a spoon and spoon the butter mixture from the bottom over the crab legs. Smoke for 30 minutes. Serve with lemon wedges.

**Servings| 4**          **Time required: 45 minutes**

# Lobster Tails

## Ingredients:

- ❖ One t. red pepper flakes
- ❖ ¼ c. lemon juice
- ❖ Two t. pepper
- ❖ Two T. chopped parsley, divided
- ❖ One minced garlic clove
- ❖ One t. salt
- ❖ Two sticks melted butter
- ❖ 4 8-ounce lobster tails

## Instructions:

i. Slice the tails along the middle, front to back. Carefully lift up the meat so that it rests on the shell. Make sure it stays attached at the base.

ii. Split the meat down the center and lay the tails on the grill.

iii. Add wood pellets to your smoker and follow your cooker's startup procedure. Preheat your smoker, with your lid closed, until it reaches 225.

iv. Mix the butter, One T. of parsley, salt, pepper, red pepper flakes, garlic, and lemon juice together. Add a T. of the mixture to each tail.

v. Cover and smoke for an hour. Baste once during cooking. The meat should turn opaque and white.

vi. Top with the remaining parsley and serve with the leftover butter.

**Servings| 4**                    **Time required: 1.5 hours**

# Oyster on the Half Shell

## Ingredients:

- ❖ One dozen shucked oysters in bottom shells
- ❖ One t. cayenne
- ❖ Two T. hot sauce
- ❖ Two minced garlic cloves
- ❖ One stick butter
- ❖ 3 T. chopped parsley
- ❖ ¼ c. parmesan
- ❖ Two T. Worcestershire sauce

## Instructions:

i.   Add wood pellets to your smoker and follow your cooker's startup procedure. Preheat your smoker, with your lid closed, until it reaches 225.

ii.  Mix the butter with all of the other ingredients, except the oysters.

iii. Place a T. of the butter on each oyster. Lay on the grill, cover, and smoke 15-20 minutes.

iv.  Serve with the rest of the butter.

**Servings| One dozen**            **Time required: One hour**

# Dijon Halibut

## *Ingredients:*

- ❖ One t. minced garlic
- ❖ Two T.s Dijon
- ❖ ¼ c. chopped cucumber
- ❖ One t. pepper
- ❖ ½ c. sweet pickle relish
- ❖ ¼ c. chopped tomato
- ❖ ½ c. mayonnaise
- ❖ ¼ c. chopped red pepper
- ❖ ¼ c. chopped onion
- ❖ Two t. salt
- ❖ ¼ EVOO
- ❖ 4 6-ounce halibut steaks

## *Instructions:*

i. Coat the fish with the oil and rub with pepper and salt. Wrap in saran wrap and refrigerate for four hours.

ii. Add wood pellets to your smoker and follow your cooker's startup procedure. Preheat your smoker, with your lid closed, until it reaches 200.

iii. Rub the chilled fish with mayonnaise.

iv. Place on the grill, cover, and smoke for two hours. It should be opaque and reach 140.

v. As the fish cooks, combine the remaining ingredients and chill until needed.

vi. Serve the fish with the mustard relish.

**Servings| 4**          **Time required: 6.5 hours**

# Citrus Trout

## *Ingredients:*

- ❖ Sliced lemon
- ❖ One T. chopped parsley
- ❖ One T. pepper
- ❖ ¼ c. salt
- ❖ ½ c. brown sugar
- ❖ One gallon orange juice
- ❖ 6-8 skin-on rainbow trout, scaled and cleaned

## *Instructions:*

i.   Fillet the fish and pat dry. Mix the pepper, salt, and sugar into the orange juice. Add in the trout, refrigerate for an hour.

ii.  Place foil on the grill and poke some holes in it. Grease.

iii. Add wood pellets to your smoker and follow your cooker's startup procedure. Preheat your smoker, with your lid closed, until it reaches 225.

iv.  Dry the trout and place on the grill, cover, and smoke an hour and a half to two hours.

v.   Serve with lemon and parsley.

**Servings| 6-8**            **Time required: 3 hours**

# Stuffed Shrimp

## *Ingredients:*

- ❖ One pound crabmeat
- ❖ One package thin-cut bacon
- ❖ Favorite barbecue rub
- ❖ 20 cleaned large shrimp

## *Instructions:*

i. Add wood pellets to your smoker and follow your cooker's startup procedure. Preheat your smoker, with your lid closed, until it reaches 40.

ii. Cut into the shrimp to create a pocket for stuffing. Place a spoonful of crab meat into each shrimp. Wrap half of a slice of bacon around the shrimp. Use a toothpick to hold in place.

iii. Rub with the barbecue rub. Let them marinate for a few minutes.

iv. Place the shrimp on the grill, cover, and cook 2-5 minutes per side. Set off the grill, and let them cool for 10-12 minutes.

v. Serve.

**Servings| 4**                 **Time required: 16 minutes**

# Parsley Lemon Shrimp

## Ingredients:

- ❖ Salt
- ❖ 3 T. chopped parsley
- ❖ ¼ c. lemon juice
- ❖ Pepper
- ❖ One pound cleaned shrimp
- ❖ ¼ c. oil

## Instructions:

i.  Add wood pellets to your smoker and follow your cooker's startup procedure. Preheat your smoker, with your lid closed, until it reaches 450.

ii.  Stir together the oil, juice, and spices and toss in the shrimp. Refrigerate for 25-35 minutes.

iii.  Place on the grill, cover, and smoke for 1-4 minutes per side.

iv.  Serve.

**Servings| 4**                    **Time required: One hour**

# Pineapple Tuna

## *Ingredients:*

- ❖ One pineapple, chunked
- ❖ One onion, chunked
- ❖ Two cubed bell peppers
- ❖ One sliced zucchini
- ❖ One pound tuna steak, cut in 4 portions
- ❖ Favorite seasonings

## *Instructions:*

i.   Add wood pellets to your smoker and follow your cooker's startup procedure. Preheat your smoker, with your lid closed, until it reaches 425.

ii.  Rub the tuna steaks with oil and let them rest for 20-25 minutes.

iii. Thread the peppers, zucchini, onion, and pineapple onto some skewers. Wooden ones should be soaked first.

iv.  Grill the kebobs, turning them every 2 minutes. After they have cooked for 5-6 minutes, place on the tuna. Each side should be grilled for about three to five mins.

v.   Serve.

**Servings| 4**                    **Time required: 35 minutes**

# Specialty Meats

## Ingredients:

- ❖ Leg of Lamb
- ❖ ½ c. canola oil
- ❖ Two T. salt
- ❖ ¼ c. EVOO
- ❖ 6-8 pound leg of lamb
- ❖ One T. pepper
- ❖ One c. red wine vinegar
- ❖ 5 minced garlic cloves
- ❖ One T. thyme
- ❖ Two T. chopped rosemary

## Instructions:

i. Mix the herbs and spices together.

ii. Tie the lamb up with butcher's string and rub generously with the oil and then the spice mix. Wrap and rest for four hours. Do not rinse the lamb once marinated.

iii. Add wood pellets to your smoker and follow your cooker's startup procedure. Preheat your smoker, with your lid closed, until it reaches 325.

iv. Mix the oil and vinegar for basting.

v. Lay the lamb on the grill, cover, and smoke 20-25 minutes per pound. Baste with the oil mixture every 30 minutes.

vi. Let the lamb rest for 15 minutes.

vii. Serve.

**Servings| 12-16**          **Time required: 4.5 hours**

# Venison Steaks

## *Ingredients:*

- ❖ 4 8-ounce venison steaks
- ❖ Two T. EVOO
- ❖ 4 minced garlic cloves
- ❖ Two t. pepper
- ❖ One T. salt
- ❖ Two t. sage

## *Instructions:*

i.   Add wood pellets to your smoker and follow your cooker's startup procedure. Preheat your smoker, with your lid closed, until it reaches 225.

ii.  Rub the steaks with the oil and spices. Place them on the grill, cover, and smoke an hour and 20 minutes, or until it reaches your desired doneness.

iii. Serve.

**Servings| 4**          **Time required: 1.5 hours**

# Quail and Fruit

## Ingredients:

- ❖ One t. cinnamon
- ❖ Two t. pepper
- ❖ ½ stick butter
- ❖ 4 peaches
- ❖ Two t. salt
- ❖ One T. sugar
- ❖ Two t. garlic powder
- ❖ 4 spatchcocked quail

## Instructions:

i.   Add wood pellets to your smoker and follow your cooker's startup procedure. Preheat your smoker, with your lid closed, until it reaches 225.

ii.  Rub the quail with the garlic, pepper, and salt. Take the pits out of the peaches.

iii. Mix together the cinnamon, butter, and sugar.

iv.  Place the quail on the grill, cover, and smoke an hour. It should reach 145. After 15 minutes, place the peaches on flesh-side down.

v.   Remove everything from the grill. Serve the peaches with the butter and quail.

**Servings| 4**                    **Time required: 1.5 hours**

# Beef Jerky

## Ingredients:

- ❖ Two t. pepper
- ❖ Two t. garlic powder
- ❖ ¼ c. Worcestershire sauce
- ❖ ¼ c. coffee
- ❖ Two pounds flank steak
- ❖ One T. celery salt
- ❖ One T. celery seeds
- ❖ ½ c. soy sauce

## Instructions:

i.   Slice the beef against the grain, ¼-inch thick.

ii.  Rub with the celery seeds and salt.

iii. Mix together the other ingredients and add in the beef. Cover and refrigerate for 12 hours.

iv.  Add wood pellets to your smoker and follow your cooker's startup procedure. Preheat your smoker, with your lid closed, until it reaches 150.

v.   Take the meat out and blot dry. Place the meat on the grill, cover, and smoke for 4-5 hours. Allow them to cool and keep refrigerated. This will last for three weeks.

**Servings| 20 slices**          **Time required: 17 hours**

# Cornish Game Hen

## Ingredients:

- ❖ One t. celery seeds
- ❖ One t. pepper
- ❖ Two t. salt
- ❖ EVOO
- ❖ 4 Cornish game hens

## Instructions:

i.   Add wood pellets to your smoker and follow your cooker's startup procedure. Preheat your smoker, with your lid closed, until it reaches 275.

ii.  Rub the hens with oil and rub with the seasonings. Place on the grill, cover, and smoke for 2-3 hours. They should reach 170.

iii. Serve.

**Servings| 4**              **Time required: 3 hours**

# Bison Burgers

## Ingredients:

- ❖ Two pounds ground bison
- ❖ Two T. steak seasoning
- ❖ 6 ciabatta rolls
- ❖ 6 slices Swiss cheese
- ❖ One minced onion
- ❖ ½ stick butter

## Instructions:

i. Add wood pellets to your smoker and follow your cooker's startup procedure. Preheat your smoker, with your lid closed, until it reaches 425.

ii. Mix the bison and the steak seasoning. Form the meat into six patties and make an indention of your thumb in the center.

iii. Place the butter and onion on a baking sheet on the grill. Cook for five minutes. Lay the patties on the onions with the indention-side down.

iv. Cover and smoke for 6-7 minutes. Flip and cover with the onions. Cook for another 6-7 minutes. Top with the cheese during the last few minutes.

v. Toast the rolls and add on the burgers and top with your favorite toppings.

vi. Serve.

**Servings| 6**            **Time required: 45 minutes**

# Stuffed Duck

## Ingredients:

- ❖ ½ t. thyme
- ❖ One t. chopped parsley
- ❖ One c. sliced mushrooms
- ❖ 4 pounds duck
- ❖ Pepper
- ❖ Salt
- ❖ ¼ c. butter

## Instructions:

i.   Mix the mushrooms into the herbs and spices. Stuff the duck with the mushroom mixture.

ii.  Add wood pellets to your smoker and follow your cooker's startup procedure. Preheat your smoker, with your lid closed, until it reaches 350.

iii. Lay the duck on the grill, cover, and cook for an hour and a half.

iv.  Serve.

**Servings| 6**           **Time required: Two hours**

# Rabbit with Garlic and Rosemary

## Ingredients:

- ❖ Pepper
- ❖ Salt
- ❖ ¼ c. oil
- ❖ One lemon, juiced
- ❖ Two T. crushed rosemary
- ❖ Two minced garlic cloves
- ❖ Two pounds rabbit

## Instructions:

i.  Don't roast the rabbit whole. Section it out into pieces.

ii.  Mix the lemon juice, pepper, salt, oil, rosemary, and garlic. Rub the mixture on the rabbit pieces.

iii.  Add wood pellets to your smoker and follow your cooker's startup procedure. Preheat your smoker, with your lid closed, until it reaches 300.

iv.  Lay the rabbit out on the grill, cover, and smoke for 12-15 minutes per side.

v.  Serve.

**Servings| 4**          **Time required: 1.5 hours**

# Drunken Goose

## *Ingredients:*

- ❖ 1 ½ t. Worcestershire sauce
- ❖ Salt
- ❖ ½ t. paprika
- ❖ One t. garlic powder
- ❖ 4 goose breasts
- ❖ Pepper
- ❖ Two c. beer

## *Instructions:*

i.   Marinate the goose in the beer, pepper, salt, paprika, garlic powder, and Worcestershire sauce. Marinate for two hours. Remove and pat dry.

ii.  Add wood pellets to your smoker and follow your cooker's startup procedure. Preheat your smoker, with your lid closed, until it reaches 300.

iii. Place the goose on the grill, cover, and smoke for an hour. It should reach 165.

iv.  Serve.

**Servings| 4**            **Time required: 3 hours**

# Brown Sugar Lamb Chops

## Ingredients:

- ❖ Pepper
- ❖ One t. garlic powder
- ❖ Salt
- ❖ Two t. tarragon
- ❖ One t. cinnamon
- ❖ ¼ c. brown sugar
- ❖ 4 lamb chops
- ❖ Two t. ginger

## Instructions:

i.   Combine the salt, garlic powder, pepper, cinnamon, tarragon, ginger, and sugar. Coat the lamb chops in the mixture and chill for two hours.

ii.  Add wood pellets to your smoker and follow your cooker's startup procedure. Preheat your smoker, with your lid closed, until it reaches 450.

iii. Place the chops on the grill, cover, and smoke for 10-15 minutes per side.

iv.  Serve.

**Servings| 4**            **Time required: 2.5 hours**

# Smoke Gyro

## Ingredients:

- ❖ One chopped tomato, for serving
- ❖ One thinly-sliced small onion, for serving
- ❖ One pound ground lamb
- ❖ Tzatziki sauce, for serving
- ❖ 4-6 pocketless pitas
- ❖ One t. ground black pepper
- ❖ Two T. chopped oregano
- ❖ One T. minced garlic
- ❖ One T. onion powder
- ❖ Two t. salt

## Instructions:

i.  Combine together in a mixing dish the lamb, salt, pepper, oregano, garlic, and onion powder. Place it in the refrigerator. Allow all of this to marinate overnight.

ii. Add wood pellets to your smoker and follow your cooker's startup procedure. Preheat your smoker, with your lid closed, until it reaches 300.

iii. Take the mixture out of the refrigerator and using aluminum foil or a Frogmat, roll and shape the mixture into a rectangular loaf. It should be about five inches wide and eight inches long.

iv. Lay the loaf right on the grill. Close your grill's lid and allow the meat to smoke for 35 minutes. The meat needs to reach 155 to be considered done.

v.     Take the loaf off of the heat and turn the temperature up to 450.

vi.    Slice the lamb loaf into eighth-inch thick slices and lay them out on a piece of aluminum foil or on a Frogmat.

vii.   Place this back on your grill and close your grill's lid. Allow this to continue to cook for two to four minutes. The edges should be crispy.

viii.  Once the meat is done, place the pits on the smoker and allow them to warm up. Add the lamb, sliced onion, chopped tomato, and tzatziki sauce on the gyro and enjoy.

**Servings| 4-6          Time required: 10 hours**

# Grilled Lasagna

## Ingredients:

- ❖ 16 ounces package dry lasagna noodles
- ❖ cooking spray
- ❖ One beaten egg
- ❖ ½ c. grated parmesan
- ❖ 3 c. shredded mozzarella, divided
- ❖ 15 ounces ricotta
- ❖ One diced medium onion
- ❖ One diced bell pepper
- ❖ One T. minced garlic
- ❖ One T. dried oregano
- ❖ 15-ounce can tomato sauce
- ❖ One T. dried basil
- ❖ ½ pound ground pork sausage
- ❖ Two 14.5-ounce cans diced tomatoes
- ❖ ½ pound ground beef

## Instructions:

i.  Using your stove top, place the pork sausage and beef in a skillet and cook them for five to seven minutes, or until it has browned up. Make sure that you break the meat up into crumbles.

ii. Take the meat off of the heat and remove any fat that may have accumulated. Mix in the diced tomatoes, tomato sauce, oregano, basil, garlic, bell pepper, and onion.

iii.   Add wood pellets to your smoker and follow your cooker's startup procedure. Preheat your smoker, with your lid closed, until it reaches 375.

iv.   Mix together the egg, parmesan, a cup of the mozzarella, and the ricotta.

v.   Grease a 3-quart aluminum pan and spread half of a cup of the meat sauce into the pan's bottom.

vi.   Dip the lasagna in some water until they soften.

vii.   On the meat's top, a third of the noodles should be placed. Cover them with a half c. of sauce.

viii.   Continue to make your layers as follows: a c. of the cheese mixture, a c. of sauce, ½ c. of mozzarella, third of the noodles, remaining cheese mixture, a c. of sauce, ½ c. of mozzarella, and the rest of the noodles. Top the lasagna with the rest of the sauce.

ix.   Use a foil to cover the pan. The pan should be placed on the grill. Close the grill's lid and let them cook for 30 minutes.

x.   Take the foil off and top the lasagna with the rest of the mozzarella. Allow the lasagna to continue to cook for 15-20 minutes. It should be bubbly.

**xi.**   For a minimum of 15 minutes, let it rest before serving.

**Servings| 10-12**                    **Time required: Two hours**

# Lamb Skewers

## Ingredients:

- ❖ One lemon, juiced
- ❖ Two crushed garlic cloves
- ❖ Two chopped red onions
- ❖ One t. chopped thyme
- ❖ Pepper
- ❖ Salt
- ❖ One t. oregano
- ❖ 1/3 c. oil
- ❖ ½ t. cumin
- ❖ Two pounds cubed lamb leg

## Instructions:

i. Refrigerate the chunked lamb.

ii. The remaining ingredients should be mixed together. Add in the meat. Refrigerate overnight.

iii. Pat the meat dry and thread onto some metal or wooden skewers. Wooden skewers should be soaked in water.

iv. Add wood pellets to your smoker and follow your cooker's startup procedure. Preheat your smoker, with your lid closed, until it reaches 450.

v. Grill, covered, for 4-6 minutes on each side.

vi. Serve.

**Servings| 6**                    **Time required: 25 minutes**

# Vegetables and Sides

## *Ingredients:*

- ❖ Spaghetti Squash Scampi
- ❖ One t. pepper
- ❖ Two T. EVOO
- ❖ One t. salt
- ❖ One spaghetti squash
- ❖ Two t. garlic powder

Sauce:

- ❖ One T. minced garlic
- ❖ One t. red pepper flakes
- ❖ ½ t. pepper
- ❖ ½ t. salt
- ❖ Two t. chopped parsley
- ❖ ½ c. white wine
- ❖ ½ stick butter

## *Instructions:*

i.   Add wood pellets to your smoker and follow your cooker's startup procedure. Preheat your smoker, with your lid closed, until it reaches 375.

ii.   Cut the ends off the squash, slice lengthwise, and scoop out the seeds. Rub with olive and sprinkle with garlic, pepper, and salt.

iii.   Place with the cut side up, cover, and smoke for 40 minutes.

iv.   Add all of the sauce ingredients to a pot and cook heated through. Lower the heat and keep warm.

v.    Take the squash off the heat and shred the flesh out with a fork. Mix the squash "noodles" in the sauce.

vi.   Serve.

**Servings| 4**                    **Time required: One hour**

# Jalapeno Poppers

## Ingredients:

- ❖ One pound pre-cooked bacon
- ❖ One t. salt
- ❖ 18 large jalapenos, cut lengthwise and seeded
- ❖ One t. garlic powder
- ❖ ¼ c. chopped scallions
- ❖ One t. Chile powder
- ❖ ½ c. shredded cheddar
- ❖ 8 ounces cream cheese

## Instructions:

i. Add wood pellets to your smoker and follow your cooker's startup procedure. Preheat your smoker, with your lid closed, until it reaches 350. Place foil on a baking sheet.

ii. Mix together the salt, garlic powder, Chile powder, scallions, cheddar, and cream cheese. Stuff this into the jalapenos. Wrap the bacon around the jalapenos. Place them on the baking sheet.

iii. Lay them on the grill, cover, and smoke for 30 minutes. Allow them to sit for three to five minutes.

iv. Serve.

**Servings| 10-12**                    **Time required: 50 minutes**

# Garlic Eggplant

## Ingredients:

- ❖ Salt
- ❖ Parsley
- ❖ 4 cloves minced garlic
- ❖ ½ c. EVOO
- ❖ Juice of one lemon
- ❖ Two pounds eggplant, sliced round

## Instructions:

i.   Put the sliced eggplants into a colander, add in the salt and lemon juice and allow to set for 20 minutes.

ii.  Add wood pellets to your smoker and follow your cooker's startup procedure. Preheat your smoker, with your lid closed, until it reaches 160.

iii. Whisk together the salt, garlic, and olive oil. Pour this mixture on the eggplant and coat well.

iv.  For about 15 mins., grill the eggplant. Flip them only once. Cook an additional 10 minutes. Sprinkle with parsley, enjoy.

**Servings| 6**                    **Time required: 35 minutes**

# Garlic Oregano Asparagus

## Ingredients:

- ❖ Pepper
- ❖ One t. cayenne pepper
- ❖ Chopped thyme
- ❖ 1/3 c. olive oil
- ❖ One T. oregano
- ❖ Zest of one lemon
- ❖ Juice of one lemon
- ❖ 3 cloves minced garlic
- ❖ One pound asparagus
- ❖ Salt

## Instructions:

i.   Cut the bottom inch off the asparagus. Place in a large container.

ii.  Put the thyme, pepper, salt, cayenne pepper, oregano, lemon zest, lemon juice, garlic, olive oil. Whisk to combine. Pour this over the asparagus.

iii. Add wood pellets to your smoker and follow your cooker's startup procedure. Preheat your smoker, with your lid closed, until it reaches2.

iv.  Place asparagus on the grill. Cover and cook until lightly browned eight minutes, turning frequently.

**Servings| 4**             **Time required: 30 minutes**

# Balsamic Honey Sweet Onions

## Ingredients:

- ❖ Pepper
- ❖ ¼ c. Dijon mustard
- ❖ T. chopped thyme
- ❖ Salt
- ❖ ¼ c. honey
- ❖ Two pounds sweet onions
- ❖ One c. balsamic vinegar
- ❖ ¼ c. olive oil

## Instructions:

i.   Peel and trim the onions. Slice them into half-inch rounds. Insert a toothpick into each slice to keep the rings together. Place into a shallow dish.

ii.  Mix the pepper, salt, thyme, mustard, honey, balsamic vinegar, and olive oil together. Pour this over the onions.

iii. Add wood pellets to your smoker and follow your cooker's startup procedure. Preheat your smoker, with your lid closed, until it reaches 400.

iv.  Put the onions on the grill and grill for ten minutes. Once they are cooked, place onto a serving platter and gently remove the toothpicks.

**Servings|6**             **Time required: 35 minutes**

# Herbed Potatoes

## *Ingredients:*

- ❖ Pepper
- ❖ Salt
- ❖ ¼ c. olive oil
- ❖ Chopped rosemary
- ❖ One T. chopped oregano
- ❖ One chopped shallot
- ❖ Two pounds potatoes

## *Instructions:*

i.   Make sure the potatoes are very clean and dry. Cut the potatoes into wedges. Put into a large container.

ii.   Add wood pellets to your smoker and follow your cooker's startup procedure. Preheat your smoker, with your lid closed, until it reaches 225.

iii.   Put the pepper, salt, rosemary, oregano, shallot, and olive oil into a bowl. Whisk to combine. Brush this mixture over the potatoes generously. Put potatoes on the grill.

iv.   Close lid and cook for one hour and 15 minutes without turning them over. Once they are fork tender, take off from the grill and adjust the seasonings if needed.

**Servings| 6**          **Time required: 1 hour 30 minutes**

# Beet Salad

## *Ingredients:*

- ❖ Pepper
- ❖ Salt
- ❖ 4 oz. goat cheese
- ❖ 1/3 c. almonds
- ❖ Two t. Dijon mustard
- ❖ ½ c. olive oil
- ❖ ½ c. balsamic vinegar
- ❖ 6 large beets
- ❖ 4 oz. baby arugula

## *Instructions:*

i. Slice beets in half. Put into a large saucepan. Pour enough water in the saucepan until it covers the beets by one inch. Add in one T. salt.

ii. Boil until the beets are tender.

iii. Add wood pellets to your smoker and follow your cooker's startup procedure. Preheat your smoker, with your lid closed, until it reaches 350.

iv. Place the beets onto the grill. Smoke for 30 minutes. Take off from the grill and cut into wedges. Place into a bowl.

v. Put one t. pepper, Dijon mustard, Two t. salt, olive oil, and balsamic vinegar in a bowl and whisk together. Set to the side.

vi.  Pour half this mixture over beet wedges and toss to coat. Drizzle the arugula with the remaining dressing and adjust seasonings if needed.

vii.  Use a serving platter to serve the two mixtures. Drizzle them with almonds and goat cheese.

**Servings| 6**          **Time required: 1 hour 15 minutes**

# Brussels Sprouts

## *Ingredients:*

- ❖ Pepper
- ❖ Salt
- ❖ One pound Brussels sprouts
- ❖ Two T. olive oil
- ❖ One t. garlic salt

## *Instructions:*

i. Add wood pellets to your smoker and follow your cooker's startup procedure. Preheat your smoker, with your lid closed, until it reaches 400.

ii. While the smoker is preheating, let's prep the vegetables. Wash and rinse the Brussels sprouts. Cut off the ends of the sprouts. Cut a small X onto the bottom end. Continue until all sprouts are prepped. Put them into a large bowl.

iii. Coat the sprouts in oil. Sprinkle with seasonings above. You can also add others seasoning and spices you like. Sprouts are very forgiving when it comes to seasonings.

iv. Spray grill with cooking spray and place the sprouts onto the grill in a single layer.

v. Smoke for 30 minutes and serve.

**Servings| 4**          **Time required: 1 hour**

# BLT Pasta Salad

## Ingredients:

- ❖ Two chopped tomatoes
- ❖ 16 ounces cooked bowtie pasta
- ❖ One pound thick-cut bacon
- ❖ One head shredded lettuce
- ❖ One t. garlic powder
- ❖ ½ c. Italian dressing
- ❖ One t. salt
- ❖ One T. chopped basil
- ❖ ½ c. ranch dressing
- ❖ One t. pepper
- ❖ ½ c. chopped scallions

## Instructions:

i. Add wood pellets to your smoker and follow your cooker's startup procedure. Preheat your smoker, with your lid closed, until it reaches 225.

ii. Grill the bacon for 30-45 minutes. Flip at the 20 minutes mark.

iii. Chop the bacon. Except for the lettuce, toss everything together. Refrigerate until you are ready to serve.

iv. Toss in the lettuce before serving.

v. Serve.

**Servings| 10-12**                    **Time required: One hour**

# Baked Beans

## Ingredients:

- ❖ ½ pound thick-cut bacon, quartered
- ❖ One large bell pepper, sliced
- ❖ Butter, for greasing
- ❖ 3 T. yellow mustard
- ❖ ½ c. light brown sugar
- ❖ One c. barbecue sauce
- ❖ One large chopped onion
- ❖ ¼ c. Worcestershire sauce
- ❖ 3 28-ounce cans baked beans

## Instructions:

i. Add wood pellets to your smoker and follow your cooker's startup procedure. Preheat your smoker, with your lid closed, until it reaches 300.

ii. Combine the mustard, Worcestershire sauce, sugar, barbecue sauce, onion, and beans. Grease a 9" x 13" pan. Pour in the beans and top with the rings of pepper and bacon pieces.

iii. Place a layer of foil on the grill and lay the pan on top. Cover and cook for two and a half to three hours. It should be thick and bubbly.

iv. Allow to rest for five minutes. Serve.

**Servings| 12-15**          **Time required: 3 hours**

# Sweet Onion Bake

## *Ingredients:*

- ❖ Butter, for greasing
- ❖ One c. parmesan
- ❖ 4 chicken bouillon cubes
- ❖ One stick melted butter
- ❖ 4 large sweet onions

## *Instructions:*

i.   Add wood pellets to your smoker and follow your cooker's startup procedure. Preheat your smoker, with your lid closed, until it reaches 350.

ii.  Butter a baking pan. Peel and quarter the onions and separate out the petals.

iii. Spread them out on the pan and pour the melted butter. The bouillon should be crushed before sprinkling them on top of the onion. Top with cheese.

iv.  Grill for 30 minutes. Remove and cover with foil. Poke holes in the foil to vent.

v.   Put back on the grill, cover, and smoke for 30 to 45 minutes. Uncover, stir, and serve.

**Servings| 6-8**          **Time required: 1.5 hours**

# Brussels Sprout Bites

## *Ingredients:*

- ❖ Two t. minced garlic
- ❖ ¼ c. chopped cilantro
- ❖ ¼ c. EVOO
- ❖ ¼ c. balsamic vinegar
- ❖ One T. Cajun seasoning
- ❖ ½ pound bacon
- ❖ One pound Brussels sprouts, wilted and trimmed

## *Instructions:*

i.   Soak some long toothpicks in water for 15 minutes

ii.  Add wood pellets to your smoker and follow your cooker's startup procedure. Preheat your smoker, with your lid closed, until it reaches 300.

iii. Wrap the Brussels sprouts with a half slice of bacon and secure with a toothpick.

iv.  Combine the Cajun seasoning and brown sugar and coat the sprouts with the sugar mixture.

v.   Lay on a baking sheet. Place on the grill, cover, and smoke for 45 minutes to an hour. Turn as needed. The bacon should crisp up.

vi.  Mix the garlic, cilantro, oil, and vinegar together.

vii. Place the bites on a plate and serve with the balsamic sauce.

viii. Serve.

**Servings| 4-6**                    **Time required: One hour**

# Bunny Dogs

## *Ingredients:*

- ❖ 8 hot dog buns
- ❖ pepper
- ❖ Salt
- ❖ Butter, for greasing
- ❖ ¼ c. yellow mustard
- ❖ ¼ c. honey
- ❖ 8 hot dog-sized peeled carrots

## *Instructions:*

i.    Remove the stems and slice the carrots in half lengthwise.

ii.   Mix the mustard and honey together.

iii.  Add wood pellets to your smoker and follow your cooker's startup procedure. Preheat your smoker, with your lid closed, until it reaches 375.

iv.   Place foil on a baking pan and spray with nonstick spray. Brush the carrots with the honey sauce and sprinkle with some pepper and salt and lay on the baking sheet.

v.    Cover them after placing them on the grill. For 35 to 40 mins., grill them. They should be tender and browned.

vi.   Toast the buns and top with two carrot slices and some relish

vii.  Serve.

**Servings| 8**                    **Time required: One hour**

# Sweet Potato Chips

## Ingredients:

- ❖ ½ t. cayenne
- ❖ One t. pepper
- ❖ One t. cinnamon
- ❖ Two sweet potatoes
- ❖ One T. salt
- ❖ ¼ c. EVOO
- ❖ One T. + Two t. cornstarch
- ❖ One quart warm water
- ❖ One T. brown sugar

## Instructions:

i.   Slice the potatoes.

ii.  Place the warm water in a bowl with a T. of cornstarch. Add the potato slices and soak for 15 to 20 minutes.

iii. Add wood pellets to your smoker and follow your cooker's startup procedure. Preheat your smoker, with your lid closed, until it reaches 375.

iv.  Drain the potatoes and place them on a perforated pizza pan. Brush with olive oil.

v.   Mix the cayenne, pepper, cinnamon, brown sugar, salt, and the reaming cornstarch. Sprinkle this over the potatoes. Make sure to coat both sides.

vi.  Grill for 35-45 minutes. Flip after 20 minutes.

vii. Keep in an airtight container.

**Servings| 2-3**          **Time required: 1.5 hours**

# Roasted Okra

## *Ingredients:*

- ❖ Butter, for greasing
- ❖ Two t. pepper
- ❖ Two T. EVOO
- ❖ Two t. seasoned salt
- ❖ One pound whole okra

## *Instructions:*

i. Add wood pellets to your smoker and follow your cooker's startup procedure. Preheat your smoker, with your lid closed, until it reaches 400.

ii. Place foil on a baking pan and grease.

iii. Place the okra on the pan and drizzle it with oil. Turn to coat. Season with pepper and salt.

iv. Grill for 30 minutes.

v. Serve.

**Servings| 3-4**             **Time required: 40 minutes**

# Twice-Smoked Potatoes

## Ingredients:

- ❖ 12 ounces heated evaporated milk
- ❖ 8 potatoes
- ❖ One c. shredded cheddar
- ❖ Pepper
- ❖ Salt
- ❖ ¼ c. chopped scallions
- ❖ ½ pounce cooked and crumbled bacon
- ❖ One c. parmesan
- ❖ ½ c. room temp sour cream
- ❖ Two stick melted butter

## Instructions:

i. Add wood pellets to your smoker and follow your cooker's startup procedure. Preheat your smoker, with your lid closed, until it reaches 400.

ii. Poke the potatoes and lay them out on the grill to cook for 1 hour 15 minutes. They should be cooked through.

iii. Let the potatoes cool for ten minutes slice lengthwise.

iv. Remove the flesh, but leave a quarter inch shell. Place the shells on a baking sheet.

v. Beat the sour cream, butter, milk, and potatoes together until smooth. Mix in the scallions, bacon, and parmesan. Add some pepper and salt.

vi. Stuff the potato shells and top with cheddar.

vii.    Place on grill, cover, and cook for 20 minutes

viii.   Serve.

**Servings| 16**                    **Time required: Two hours**

# Mexican Street Corn

## *Ingredients:*

- ❖ One c. parmesan
- ❖ ¼ c. chopped cilantro
- ❖ ½ c. mayonnaise
- ❖ ½ c. sour cream
- ❖ 4 ears corn

## *Instructions:*

i.   Add wood pellets to your smoker and follow your cooker's startup procedure. Preheat your smoker, with your lid closed, until it reaches 450.

ii.  Shuck and clean the corn. Cut four squares of foil to cover the corn.

iii. Mix together the cilantro, mayonnaise, and sour cream. Slather this on the corn. Wrap in the foil and lay them out on the grill and smoke for 12-14 minutes.

iv.  Unwrap the corn and serve topped with more cilantro and parmesan.

**Servings| 4**              **Time required: 20 minutes**

# Kale Chips

## *Ingredients:*

- ❖ Salt
- ❖ Oil
- ❖ Two bunches kale, washed and stems removed

## *Instructions:*

i. Dry the kale and place them on a baking sheet. Drizzle with and salt.

ii. Add wood pellets to your smoker and follow your cooker's startup procedure. Preheat your smoker, with your lid closed, until it reaches 250.

iii. Place the baking sheet on the grill, cover, and cook for 20 minutes.

iv. Serve.

**Servings| 4-6**          **Time required: 25 minutes**

# Butter Cabbage

## Ingredients:

- ❖ Two T. white balsamic vinegar
- ❖ One stick butter
- ❖ Two T. favorite rub
- ❖ One head cabbage

## Instructions:

i. Add wood pellets to your smoker and follow your cooker's startup procedure. Preheat your smoker, with your lid closed, until it reaches 250.

ii. Core the cabbage and remove one large leaf. Layer the inside with of the cabbage with butter and rub. Push your finger into the butter to make a hole and pour in the balsamic vinegar.

iii. Place the reserved cabbage leaf on top. Place on grill and cook for four hours.

iv. Wrap in foil and smoke for another two hours.

v. Serve.

**Servings| 4-6**          **Time required: 6 hours**

# Corn on the Cob

## Ingredients:

- ❖ One c. cojita cheese
- ❖ lime
- ❖ ¼ c. favorite rub
- ❖ ½ c. mayonnaise
- ❖ 4 ears of corn, with husks

## Instructions:

i.   Add wood pellets to your smoker and follow your cooker's startup procedure. Preheat your smoker, with your lid closed, until it reaches 300.

ii.  Lay the corn out on the grill and smoke for 20 minutes. Turn the corn every five minutes.

iii. Carefully remove the corn and pull back the husks. Brush with the mayo and sprinkle on the cheese and rub. Garnish with lime.

iv.  Serve.

**Servings| 4**                    **Time required: 20 minutes**

# Snacks, Desserts, Breads, and Extras

## Formaggi Macaroni and Cheese

### Ingredients:

- ¼ c. all-purpose flour
- ½ stick butter
- Butter, for greasing
- One pound cooked elbow macaroni
- One c. grated Parmesan
- 8 ounces cream cheese
- Two c. shredded Monterey Jack
- 3 t. garlic powder
- Two t. salt
- One t. pepper
- Two c. shredded Cheddar, divided
- 3 c. milk

### Instructions:

i.   Add the butter to a pot and melt. Mix in the flour. Stir constantly for a minute. Mix in the pepper, salt, garlic powder, and milk. Let it boil.

ii.  After lowering the heat, let it simmer for about 5 mins, or until it has thickened. Remove from the heat.

iii.  Mix in the cream cheese, parmesan, Monterey jack, and 1 ½ c. of cheddar. Stir everything until melted. Fold in the pasta.

iv.  Add wood pellets to your smoker and follow your cooker's startup procedure. Preheat your smoker, with your lid closed, until it reaches 225.

v.  Butter a 9" x 13" baking pan. Pour the macaroni mixture to the pan and lay on the grill. Cover and allow it to smoke for an hour, or until it has become bubbly. Top the macaroni with rest of the cheddar during the last

vi.  Serve.

**Servings| 8**                    **Time required: 1.5 hours**

# Spicy Barbecue Pecans

## Ingredients:

- ❖ 2 ½ t. garlic powder
- ❖ 16 ounces raw pecan halves
- ❖ One t. onion powder
- ❖ One t. pepper
- ❖ Two t. salt
- ❖ One t. dried thyme
- ❖ Butter, for greasing
- ❖ 3 T. melted butter

## Instructions:

i.   Add wood pellets to your smoker and follow your cooker's startup procedure. Preheat your smoker, with your lid closed, until it reaches 225.

ii.  Place parchment on a baking sheet and coat with some butter.

iii. Mix the thyme, salt, onion powder, pepper, garlic powder, and butter together. Add in the pecans and toss everything to coat.

iv.  Pour the nuts onto the baking pan and place them on the grill.

v.   Cover and smoke for an hour, flipping the nuts one. Make sure the nuts are toasted and heated. They should be removed from the grill. Set aside to cool and dry.

vi.  These can be kept for three weeks in an airtight container.

**Servings| Two cups**                    **Time required: One hour**

# Ice Cream Bread

## *Ingredients:*

- ❖ 1 ½ quart full-fat butter pecan ice cream, softened
- ❖ One t. salt
- ❖ Two c. semisweet chocolate chips
- ❖ One c. sugar
- ❖ One stick melted butter
- ❖ Butter, for greasing
- ❖ 4 c. self-rising flour

## *Instructions:*

i. Add wood pellets to your smoker and follow your cooker's startup procedure. Preheat your smoker, with your lid closed, until it reaches 350.

ii. Mix together the salt, sugar, flour, and ice cream with an electric mixer set to medium for two minutes.

iii. As the mixer is still running, add in the chocolate chips, beating until everything is blended.

iv. Spray a Bundt pan or tube pan with cooking spray. If you choose to use a pan that is solid, the center will take too long to cook. That's why a tube or Bundt pan works best.

v. Add the batter to your prepared pan.

vi. Set the cake on the grill, cover, and smoke for 50 minutes to an hour. A toothpick should come out clean.

vii.   Take the pan off of the grill. For 10 mins., cool the bread. Remove carefully the bread from the pan and then drizzle it with some melted butter.

**Servings| 12-16**                    **Time required: One hour**

# Blackberry Pie

## Ingredients:

- ❖ Butter, for greasing
- ❖ ½ c. all-purpose flour
- ❖ ½ c. milk
- ❖ Two pints blackberries
- ❖ Two c. sugar, divided
- ❖ One box refrigerated piecrusts
- ❖ One stick melted butter
- ❖ One stick of butter
- ❖ Vanilla ice cream

## Instructions:

i.   Add wood pellets to your smoker and follow your cooker's startup procedure. Preheat your smoker, with your lid closed, until it reaches 375.

ii.  Butter a cast iron skillet.

iii. Unroll a piecrust and lay it in the bottom and up the sides of the skillet. Use a fork to poke holes in the crust.

iv.  Lay the skillet on the grill and smoke for five mins, or until the crust is browned. Set off the grill.

v.   Mix together 1 ½ c. of sugar, the flour, and the melted butter together. Add in the blackberries and toss everything together.

vi.  The berry mixture should be added to the skillet. The milk should be added on the top afterward. Sprinkle on half of the diced butter.

vii.    Unroll the second pie crust and lay it over the skillet. You can also slice it into strips and weave it on top to make it look like a lattice. Place the rest of the diced butter over the top. Sprinkle the rest of the sugar over the crust and place it skillet back on the grill.

viii.   Lower the lid and smoke for 15 to 20 minutes or until it is browned and bubbly. You may want to cover with some foil to keep it from burning during the last few minutes of cooking. Serve the hot pie with some vanilla ice cream.

**Servings| 8**              **Time required: 40 minutes**

# S'MORES Dip

## Ingredients:

- ❖ 12 ounces semisweet chocolate chips
- ❖ ¼ c. milk
- ❖ Two T. melted salted butter
- ❖ 16 ounces marshmallows
- ❖ Apple wedges
- ❖ Graham crackers

## Instructions:

i.   Add wood pellets to your smoker and follow your cooker's startup procedure. Preheat your smoker, with your lid closed, until it reaches 450.

ii.  Put a cast iron skillet on your grill and add in the milk and melted butter. Stir together for a minute.

iii. Once it has heated up, top with the chocolate chips, making sure it makes a single layer. Place the marshmallows on top, standing them on their end and covering the chocolate.

iv.  Cover, and let it smoke for five to seven minutes. The marshmallows should be toasted lightly.

v.   Take the skillet off the heat and serve with apple wedges and graham crackers.

**Servings| 6-8**          **Time required: 15 minutes**

# Bacon Chocolate Chip Cookies

## *Ingredients:*

- ❖ 8 slices cooked and crumbled bacon
- ❖ 2 ½ t. apple cider vinegar
- ❖ One t. vanilla
- ❖ Two c. semisweet chocolate chips
- ❖ Two room temp eggs
- ❖ 1 ½ t. baking soda
- ❖ One c. granulated sugar
- ❖ ½ t. salt
- ❖ 2 ¾ c. all-purpose flour
- ❖ One c. light brown sugar
- ❖ 1 ½ stick softened butter

## *Instructions:*

i.   Mix together the flour, baking soda, and salt.

ii.  Cream the sugar and the butter together. Lower the speed. Add in the eggs, vinegar, and vanilla.

iii. Still on low, slowly add in the flour mixture, bacon pieces, and chocolate chips.

iv.  Add wood pellets to your smoker and follow your cooker's startup procedure. Preheat your smoker, with your lid closed, until it reaches 375.

v.   Place some parchment on a baking sheet and drop a teaspoonful of cookie batter on the baking sheet. Let them cook on the grill, covered, for approximately 12 minutes or until they are browned. Enjoy.

**Servings| 24 cookies**                     **Time required: 30 minutes**

# Cinnamon Sugar Pumpkin Seeds

## Ingredients:

- ❖ Two T. sugar
- ❖ seeds from a pumpkin
- ❖ One t. cinnamon
- ❖ Two T. melted butter

## Instructions:

i. Add wood pellets to your smoker and follow your cooker's startup procedure. Preheat your smoker, with your lid closed, until it reaches 350.

ii. Clean the seeds and toss them in the melted butter. Add them to the sugar and cinnamon. Spread them out on a baking sheet, place on the grill, and smoke for 25 minutes.

iii. Serve.

**Servings| 8-12**                 **Time required: 30 minutes**

# Feta Cheese Stuffed Meatballs

## Ingredients:

- ❖ Pepper
- ❖ Salt
- ❖ ¾ c. Feta cheese
- ❖ ½ t. thyme
- ❖ Two t. chopped oregano
- ❖ Zest of one lemon
- ❖ One pound ground pork
- ❖ One pound ground beef
- ❖ One T. olive oil

## Instructions:

i. Place the pepper, salt, thyme, oregano, olive oil, lemon zest, and ground meats into a large bowl.

ii. Combine thoroughly the ingredients using your hands.

iii. Cut the Feta into little cubes and begin making the meatballs. Take a half tablespoon of the meat mixture and roll it around a piece of cheese. Continue until all meat has been used.

iv. Add wood pellets to your smoker and follow your cooker's startup procedure. Preheat your smoker, with your lid closed, until it reaches 350.

v. Brush the meatballs with more olive oil and put onto the grill. Grill for ten minutes until browned.

**Servings| 6**             **Time required: 35 minutes**

# Mediterranean Meatballs

## *Ingredients:*

- ❖ Pepper
- ❖ Salt
- ❖ One t. vinegar
- ❖ Two T. olive oil
- ❖ Two eggs
- ❖ One chopped onion
- ❖ One soaked slice of bread
- ❖ ½ t. cumin
- ❖ One T. chopped basil
- ❖ 1 ½ T. chopped parsley
- ❖ 2 ½ pounds ground beef

## *Instructions:*

i. Use your hands to combine everything together until thoroughly combined. If needed, when forming meatballs, dip your hands into some water. Shape into 12 meatballs.

ii. Add wood pellets to your smoker and follow your cooker's startup procedure. Preheat your smoker, with your lid closed, until it reaches 380.

iii. Place the meatballs onto the grill and cook on all sides for eight minutes. Take off the grill and let sit for five minutes.

iv. Serve with favorite condiments or a salad.

**Servings| 6**                    **Time required: 40 minutes**

# Greek Meatballs

## *Ingredients:*

- ❖ Pepper
- ❖ Salt
- ❖ One t. thyme
- ❖ One t. cumin
- ❖ One T. oregano
- ❖ Two T. chopped parsley
- ❖ ¼ c. olive oil
- ❖ Two chopped green onions
- ❖ One T. almond flour
- ❖ Two eggs
- ❖ ½ pound ground pork
- ❖ 2 ½ pound ground beef

## *Instructions:*

i.   Mix all the ingredients together using your hands until everything is incorporated evenly. Form mixture into meatballs until all meat is used.

ii.  Add wood pellets to your smoker and follow your cooker's startup procedure. Preheat your smoker, with your lid closed, until it reaches 380.

iii. Brush the meatballs with olive oil and place onto grill. Cook for ten minutes on all sides.

**Servings| 8**            **Time required: 35 minutes**

# Turkey Jerky

## Ingredients:

- ❖ One T. Asian chili-garlic paste
- ❖ One T. curing salt
- ❖ ½ c. soy sauce
- ❖ ¼ c. water
- ❖ Two T. honey
- ❖ Two T. lime juice
- ❖ Two pounds boneless, skinless turkey breast

## Instructions:

i.   Mix together the salt, water, lime juice, chili-garlic paste, honey, and soy sauce.

ii.  Slice the turkey into thin strips. Lay the slices into a large zip-top baggie. If there is more meat that can fit into one bag, use as many as you need. Pour marinade over the turkey. Seal the bag and shake it around so that each slice gets coated with the marinade. Place the bag into the refrigerator overnight.

iii. Add wood pellets to your smoker and follow your cooker's startup procedure. Preheat your smoker, with your lid closed, until it reaches 350.

iv.  Take the sliced turkey out of the bags. Use paper towels to pat them dry. Place them evenly over the grill into one layer. Smoke the turkey for two hours. The jerky should feel dry but still chewable when done.

v.   Place into the zip-top bag to keep fresh until ready to eat.

**Servings| 8**              **Time required: 2 hours 30 minutes**

# Butternut Squash

## *Ingredients:*

- ❖ Brown sugar
- ❖ Maple syrup
- ❖ 6 T. butter
- ❖ Butternut squash

## *Instructions:*

i.   Add wood pellets to your smoker and follow your cooker's startup procedure. Preheat your smoke, with your lid closed, until it reaches 300.

ii.  Slice the squash in half, lengthwise. Clean out all the seeds and membrane.

iii. Place this cut-side down on the grill and smoke for 30 minutes. Flip the squash over and cook for another 30 minutes.

iv.  Place each half of the squash onto aluminum foil. Sprinkle each half with brown sugar and maple syrup, and put 3 T. of butter onto each. Wrap foil around to create a tight seal.

v.   Increase temperature to 400 and place onto the grill for another 35 minutes.

vi.  Carefully unwrap each half making sure to reserve juices in the bottom. Place onto serving platter and drizzle juices over each half. Use a spoon to scoop out and enjoy.

**Servings| 4-6**              **Time required: Two hours**

# Chocolate Chip Cookies

## *Ingredients:*

- ❖ 1 ½ c. chopped walnuts
- ❖ One t. vanilla
- ❖ Two c. chocolate chips
- ❖ One t. baking soda
- ❖ 2 ½ c. plain flour
- ❖ ½ t. salt
- ❖ 1 ½ stick softened butter
- ❖ Two eggs
- ❖ One c. brown sugar
- ❖ ½ c. sugar

## *Instructions:*

i.   Add wood pellets to your smoker and follow your cooker's startup procedure. Preheat your smoker, with your lid closed, until it reaches 350.

ii.  Mix together the baking soda, salt, and flour.

iii. Cream the brown sugar, sugar, and butter. Mix in the vanilla and eggs until it comes together.

iv.  Slowly add in the flour while continuing to beat. Once all flour has been incorporated, add in the chocolate chips and walnuts. Using a spoon, fold into batter.

v.   Place an aluminum foil onto grill. In an aluminum foil, drop spoonfuls of dough and bake for 17 mins.

**Servings| 12**               **Time required: 30 minutes**

# Apple Cobbler

## *Ingredients:*

- ❖ 8 Granny Smith apples
- ❖ One c. sugar
- ❖ One stick melted butter
- ❖ One t. cinnamon
- ❖ Pinch salt
- ❖ ½ c. brown sugar
- ❖ Two eggs
- ❖ Two t. baking powder
- ❖ Two c. plain flour
- ❖ 1 ½ c. sugar

## *Instructions:*

i.   Peel and quarter apples, place into a bowl. Add in the cinnamon and one c. sugar. Stir well to coat and let it set for one hour.

ii.  Add wood pellets to your smoker and follow your cooker's startup procedure. Preheat your smoker, with your lid closed, until it reaches 350.

iii. In a large bowl add the salt, baking powder, eggs, brown sugar, sugar, and flour. Mix until it forms crumbles.

iv.  Place apples into a Dutch oven. Add the crumble mixture on top and drizzle with melted butter.

v.   Place on the grill and cook for 50 minutes.

**Servings| 8**              **Time required: 1 hour 50 minutes**

# Pineapple Cake

## *Ingredients:*

- ❖ One c. sugar
- ❖ One T. baking powder
- ❖ One c. buttermilk
- ❖ Two eggs
- ❖ ½ t. salt
- ❖ One jar maraschino cherries
- ❖ One stick butter, divided
- ❖ ¾ c. brown sugar
- ❖ One can pineapple slices
- ❖ 1 ½ c. flour

## *Instructions:*

i.   Add wood pellets to your smoker and follow your cooker's startup procedure. Preheat your smoker, with your lid closed, until it reaches 350.

ii.  Take a medium-sized cast iron skillet and melt one half stick butter. Be sure to coat the entire skillet. Sprinkle brown sugar into a cast iron skillet.

iii. Lay the sliced pineapple on top of the brown sugar. Place a cherry into the middle of each pineapple ring.

iv.  Mix together the salt, baking powder, flour, and sugar. Add in the eggs, one-half stick melted butter, and buttermilk. Whisk to combine.

v.   Put the cake on the grill and cook for an hour.

vi.   Take off from the grill and let it set for ten minutes. Flip onto serving platter.

**Servings| 8**              **Time required: 1 hour 20 minutes**

# Caramel Bananas

## Ingredients:

- ❖ 1/3 c. chopped pecans
- ❖ ½ c. sweetened condensed milk
- ❖ 4 slightly green bananas
- ❖ ½ c. brown sugar
- ❖ Two T. corn syrup
- ❖ ½ c. butter

## Instructions:

i.   Add wood pellet to your smoker and follow your cooker's startup procedure. Preheat your smoker, with the lid closed, until it reaches 350.

ii.  Place the milk, corn syrup, butter, and brown sugar into a heavy saucepan and bring to boil. For five mins., simmer the mixture in low heat. Stir frequently.

iii. Place the bananas with their peels on, on the grill and let them grill for five minutes. Flip them over and cook for another five minutes. Peels will be dark and might split.

iv.  Place on serving platter. Cut the ends off the bananas and split peel down the middle. Take the peel off the bananas and spoon caramel on top. Sprinkle with pecans.

**Servings| 4**                  **Time required: 15 minutes**

# Apple Pie

## *Ingredients:*

- ❖ One frozen pie crust, thawed
- ❖ ¼ c. sugar
- ❖ ¼ c. peach preserves
- ❖ One T. cornstarch
- ❖ 5 apples, cored and sliced thin

## *Instructions:*

i.   Add wood pellet to your smoker and follow your cooker's startup procedure. Preheat your smoker, with the lid closed, until it reaches 375.

ii.  Mix the cornstarch, sugar, and apples together. Set to the side.

iii. Unroll the pie crust and put into a pie pan. Spread the peach preserves evenly on the crust. Lay the apples out onto the crust. Fold the crust over apples.

iv.  Place on baking sheet upside down on the grill. Place the pie pan on top and bake for 35 mins. Let it cool for five minutes before slicing.

**Servings| 8**                **Time required: 50 minutes**

# Pumpkin Pie

## *Ingredients:*

- ❖ 3 eggs
- ❖ 1/3 c. heavy cream
- ❖ ½ c. brown sugar
- ❖ One 15 oz. can pumpkin puree
- ❖ One 9-in pie crust in tin pie plate
- ❖ One t. pumpkin pie spice
- ❖ 4 oz. cream cheese
- ❖ Whipped topping

## *Instructions:*

i.   Add wood pellet to your smoker and follow your cooker's startup procedure. Preheat your smoker, with the lid closed, until it reaches 325.

ii.  Place the pumpkin pie spice, cream cheese, milk, pumpkin puree into a bowl and blend well. Mix an egg in at a time until all are incorporated. Pour into a pie shell.

iii. Place on the grill for 50 minutes. Edges will be firm when done. Top with whipped topping.

**Servings| 8**                **Time required: One hour**

# Sweet Plums

## Ingredients:

- ❖ ½ c. brown sugar
- ❖ ½ c. balsamic vinegar
- ❖ 10 black plums

## Instructions:

i.   Add wood pellet to your smoker and follow your cooker's startup procedure. Preheat your smoker, with the lid closed, until it reaches 350.

ii.  Cut the plums in half and remove pits.

iii. Place plums on grill cut side down and grill for ten minutes.

iv.  Place the balsamic vinegar and brown sugar into a pot and simmer for ten minutes until thick. Turn plum over and baste with balsamic vinegar mixture and cook for another five minutes.

**Servings| 10**                    **Time required: 25 minutes**

# Blueberry Bread Muffin

## Ingredients:

- ❖ Salt
- ❖ 2 ½ c. milk
- ❖ 1 ½ t. vanilla
- ❖ One t. cinnamon
- ❖ 1 ½ c. sugar
- ❖ 5 eggs
- ❖ 3 c. blueberries
- ❖ 5 c. bread, cut into one inch cubes

## Instructions:

i.   Mix together the salt, cinnamon, vanilla, sugar, milk, and eggs.

ii.  Mix the blueberries and bread together.

iii. Pour egg mixture over bread mixture and allow to set for 30 minutes. Place paper liners into a muffin tin.

iv.  Add wood pellet to your smoker and follow your cooker's startup procedure. Preheat your smoker, with the lid closed, until it reaches 225.

v.   Spoon the bread mixture into the prepared muffin tin. Sprinkle with sugar. Place on the grill for 30 minutes. Increase temperature to 350 and allow it to smoke for 25 minutes or until golden.

**Servings| 12**          **Time required: 1 hour 35 minutes**

# Peach Popsicles

## *Ingredients:*

- ❖ One c. cream, divided
- ❖ One vanilla bean
- ❖ One c. plain yogurt
- ❖ ½ c. honey
- ❖ 4 peaches

## *Instructions:*

i. Add wood pellet to your smoker and follow your cooker's startup procedure. Preheat your smoker, with the lid closed, until it reaches 450.

ii. Slice the peaches in half and remove pits. Put about two tablespoons of honey onto each cut side of the peach. Place on grill and cook for ten minutes.

iii. Take off the grill and put into a blender. Process until smooth. Put to the side.

iv. In a bowl, put vanilla, beans, honey, milk, and yogurt. Whisk until they are well-combined.

v. Place some peach puree into a popsicle mold. Layer with the yogurt mixture. Continue to layer until molds are filled ¾ of the way. Place sticks into each mold and freeze for four hours.

**Servings| 6**                    **Time required: 3 hours 15 minutes**

# Peach Cobbler

## Ingredients:

- ❖ Pinch cinnamon
- ❖ 2/3 c. flour
- ❖ 1 c. plus one T. sugar
- ❖ ¾ t. baking powder
- ❖ ½ t. vanilla
- ❖ Two T. melted butter
- ❖ Salt
- ❖ 3 pounds sliced peaches
- ❖ ½ c. butter, cubed
- ❖ One egg

## Instructions:

i.   Add wood pellet to your smoker and follow your cooker's startup procedure. Preheat your smoker, with the lid closed, until it reaches 350.

ii.  Place the two T. melted butter into a cast iron skillet. Put the peaches into the skillet.

iii. Combine the flour, cinnamon, salt, and baking powder.

iv.  In a separate bowl, cream the butter, vanilla, ½ c. sugar, and egg. Slowly fold in the flour. Pour the batter over the peaches and top with one T. sugar.

v.   Place the skillet on the grill and bake for 40 minutes.

**Servings| 8**                    **Time required: One hour**

# Brownies

## *Ingredients:*

- ❖ 4 oz. unsweetened baker's chocolate
- ❖ One c. flour
- ❖ ¼ t. salt
- ❖ One t. vanilla
- ❖ Two c. sugar
- ❖ 4 eggs
- ❖ ½ c. butter

## *Instructions:*

i.   Add wood pellet to your smoker and follow your cooker's startup procedure. Preheat your smoker, with the lid closed, until it reaches 350.

ii.  Melt the butter and chocolate together.

iii. Beat together the vanilla, eggs, and sugar until fluffy and light. Pour chocolate into this mixture and stir until combined.

iv.  Mix in the flour, and again, mix until combined. Put batter into a 13" x 9" baking dish and place on the lower rack of grill. Bake for 25 minutes with lid closed. Slice into squares.

**Servings| 12**               **Time required: 35 minutes**

# Roasted Pumpkin Seeds

## Ingredients:

- ❖ Seeds from a pumpkin
- ❖ Favorite dry rub
- ❖ Two t. melted butter

## Instructions:

i. Add wood pellets to your smoker and follow your cooker's startup procedure. Preheat your smoker, with your lid closed, until it reaches 300.

ii. Clean the seeds and dry. Toss them in the melted butter and then toss in the dry rub. Spread them across a baking sheet. Place on the grill and cook for 45 minutes.

**Servings| 8-12**                    **Time required: 50 minutes**

# Sweet Cheese Muffins

## *Ingredients:*

- ❖ Two room temp beaten eggs
- ❖ 2 ¼ c. buttermilk
- ❖ One c. self-rising flour
- ❖ ¼ c. packed brown sugar
- ❖ 3 ½ c. shredded cheddar
- ❖ 1 ½ stick softened butter
- ❖ One stick melted butter
- ❖ Butter, for greasing
- ❖ One package corn muffin mix
- ❖ One package butter cake mix

## *Instructions:*

i.  Add wood pellets to your smoker and follow your cooker's startup procedure. Preheat your smoker, with your lid closed, until it reaches 375.

ii.  Mix together the flour, corn muffin mix, and cake mix.

iii.  Slice up the softened butter and cut into the flour mixture.

iv.  Beat together the buttermilk and the eggs and mix into the flour mixture until everything has come together.

v.  Grease three 12-c. mini muffin pans. Spoon in a quarter cup of the batter into the cup

vi.  Place them on the grill, cover, and smoke for 12 to 15 minutes. Make sure that you monitor the muffins closely. They should be lightly browned.

vii.   As they are cooking, mix together the brown sugar and the melted butter.

viii.  Take the muffins off of the grill and brush with the sweet butter. Serve.

**Servings| 36 mini muffins**                    **Time required: 30 minutes**

# Sopapilla Cheesecake

## Ingredients:

- ❖ Two t. vanilla
- ❖ Two T. butter
- ❖ 24-ounces cream cheese
- ❖ Two cans crescent roll dough
- ❖ Two c. sugar
- ❖ ½ c. melted butter

## Instructions:

i.   Rub a 9" x 13" baking dish with two T. of butter.

ii.  Add wood pellets to your smoker and follow your cooker's startup procedure. Preheat your smoker, with your lid closed, until it reaches 350.

iii. Beat together the 1 ½ c. sugar, vanilla, and cream cheese.

iv.  Open a can of crescent dough and lay it into the baking dish. Pinch the seams together. Top with the cream cheese and then place the second can of dough over the top. Again, pinch the seams together.

v.   Pour the melted butter on top and sprinkle with remaining sugar.

vi.  Place on the grill, cover, and cook for 40-50 mins. Before serving, cool it for about 10 mins.

**Servings| 8-12**              **Time required: One hour**

# Bacon Cheeseball

## Ingredients:

- ❖ Salt
- ❖ One c. shredded cheddar
- ❖ ½ pound sliced bacon
- ❖ ¼ c. sour cream
- ❖ One t. garlic powder
- ❖ 4 T. chopped onion
- ❖ One pound cream cheese

## Instructions:

i.   Add wood pellets to your smoker and follow your cooker's startup procedure. Preheat your smoker, with your lid closed, until it reaches 180.

ii.   Lay the cream cheese and sour cream in a baking dish. Cook for 20 mins in the grill, covered. Remove and turn the grill to 350.

iii.   Add the bacon and grill for 15-20 minutes. Remove and cool.

iv.   Mix the cream cheese, sour cream, and the other ingredients together in a food processor. Place on plastic wrap and form into a ball. Chill until firm and roll in chopped bacon.

v.   Serve.

**Servings| 8-12**              **Time required: 45 minutes**

# Cinnamon Almonds

## *Ingredients:*

- ❖ ½ c. brown sugar
- ❖ Salt
- ❖ One egg white
- ❖ One T. cinnamon
- ❖ ½ c. sugar
- ❖ One pound almonds

## *Instructions:*

i. Beat the egg white until frothy. Mix in the salt, cinnamon, and sugars. Toss in the almonds to coat.

ii. Add wood pellets to your smoker and follow your cooker's startup procedure. Preheat your smoker, with your lid closed, until it reaches 225.

iii. Lay the almonds on a cookie sheet and place on the grill, cover. Cook for 90 minutes. Stir every ten minutes.

iv. Serve.

**Servings| 4-6**          **Time required: 1.5 hours**

# Pomegranate Lemonade

## *Ingredients:*

- ❖ One c. pomegranate seeds
- ❖ One small bottle pom juice
- ❖ 2-3 smoked ice cubes
- ❖ 4-ounce lemonade
- ❖ 1.5-ounces vodka

## *Instructions:*

i.   Add wood pellets to your smoker and follow your cooker's startup procedure. Preheat your smoker, with your lid closed, until it reaches 180.

ii.  To make the ice cubes, add the pom juice and pomegranate seeds to a sheet pan and smoke for 45 minutes. Remove and chill. Pour into an ice mold and freeze.

iii. Place the ice in a tall glass and add in the lemonade and vodka.

iv.  Serve.

**Servings| One**                    **Time required: 45 minutes**

# Apple Cider

## *Ingredients:*

- ❖ Two pieces orange peel
- ❖ 3 star anise
- ❖ Two pieces lemon peel
- ❖ Two cinnamon sticks
- ❖ 32-ounces apple cider

## *Instructions:*

i.   Add wood pellets to your smoker and follow your cooker's startup procedure. Preheat your smoker, with your lid closed, to smoke.

ii.  Mix everything together in a shallow dish. Place it on the grill, cover, and smoke for 30 minutes.

iii. Remove and serve in four glasses.

**Servings| 2-4**              **Time required: 30 minutes**

# Green Beans with Bacon

## Ingredients:

- ❖ Two minced garlic cloves
- ❖ 4 strips of diced bacon
- ❖ One t. salt
- ❖ 1 ½ pound trimmed green beans
- ❖ 4 T. oil

## Instructions:

i.   Add wood pellets to your smoker and follow your cooker's startup procedure. Preheat your smoker, with your lid closed, until it reaches 400.

ii.  Toss everything together and place on a sheet tray. Place on the grill, cover, and roast for 20 minutes.

iii. Serve.

**Servings| 4-6**          **Time required: 20 minutes**

# Bacon Wrapped Tomatoes

## *Ingredients:*

- ❖ 10 slices bacon
- ❖ Pepper
- ❖ 20 cherry tomatoes

## *Instructions:*

i.    Add wood pellets to your smoker and follow your cooker's startup procedure. Preheat your smoker, with your lid closed, to high.

ii.   Slice the bacon in half and wrap a half around each of the tomatoes. Use a toothpick to secure. In a baking sheet, lay the slices of bacon. Sprinkle with pepper.

iii.  Place on grill, cover, and cook for 25 minutes. Serve with basil and balsamic vinegar.

**Servings| 4-6**            **Time required: 40 minutes**

# Parmesan Artichoke Mushrooms

## Ingredients:

- ❖ 1/3 c. parmesan
- ❖ ¼ c. mayonnaise
- ❖ 6.5-ounces chopped artichoke hearts
- ❖ ½ t. garlic salt
- ❖ Paprika
- ❖ 8 medium mushroom caps

## Instructions:

i.   Clean the mushrooms and discard stems. Scoop out the gills. Mix all of the other ingredients together and stuff into the mushroom caps. Dust with paprika.

ii.  Lay on a baking dish.

iii. Add wood pellets to your smoker and follow your cooker's startup procedure. Preheat your smoker, with your lid closed, until it reaches 350.

iv.  Place the dish on the grill, cover, and cook for 25-30 minutes.

v.   Serve.

**Servings| 8-12**                    **Time required: 45 minutes**

# Steak Fries

## *Ingredients:*

- ❖ One t. melted butter
- ❖ One t. onion powder
- ❖ Two T. canola oil
- ❖ 3 t. salt
- ❖ 3 crushed garlic cloves
- ❖ One t. pepper
- ❖ 5 large potatoes

## *Instructions:*

i.   Wash the potatoes and slice into fires. Toss them in the oil and seasonings.

ii.  Add wood pellets to your smoker and follow your cooker's startup procedure. Preheat your smoker, with your lid closed, until it reaches 450.

iii. Place the fires on the grill, turning them to get the grill marks. Allow this to cook for ten minutes.

iv.  Serve.

**Servings| 6-8**          **Time required: 35 minutes**

# Buffalo Fries

## *Ingredients:*

- ❖ Pepper
- ❖ ½ c. hot sauce
- ❖ Salt
- ❖ 6 potatoes
- ❖ Two c. blue cheese dressing
- ❖ 4 bone-in chicken breasts

## *Instructions:*

i.  Add wood pellets to your smoker and follow your cooker's startup procedure. Preheat your smoker, with your lid closed, until it reaches 325.

ii.  Add some pepper and salt to the chicken and smoke for 25-30 minutes. Shred the chicken.

iii.  Mix the hot sauce and dressing together.

iv.  Slice the potatoes into fries and grill 10-20 minutes. Season with salt. Place the fries on a platter and drizzle with the dressing and then add the chicken.

v.  Serve.

**Servings| 4-6**          **Time required: 50 minutes**

# Turkey Stuffing Bacon Balls

## *Ingredients:*

- ❖ One can cranberry sauce
- ❖ 3 c. cooked stuffing
- ❖ One jalapeno, diced
- ❖ 6 slices bacon
- ❖ One c. shredded turkey

## *Instructions:*

i. In a pot, boil the mixture of cranberry sauce and jalapeno. Lower to a simmer for four to five minutes.

ii. Add wood pellets to your smoker and follow your cooker's startup procedure. Preheat your smoker, with your lid closed, until it reaches 375.

iii. Form some stuffing into a ball and make a pocket with your thumb. Fill with the shredded turkey and cover over with stuffing.

iv. Wrap with a half slice of bacon. Continue until stuffing, turkey, and bacon are used.

v. Place on the grill, cover, and cook for 25-30 minutes. Serve the cranberry sauce.

**Servings| 8-12**                    **Time required: 30 minutes**

# Bacon and Herb Popovers

## Ingredients:

- ❖ One T. chopped herbs
- ❖ Two c. flour
- ❖ ½ c. butter
- ❖ One t. salt
- ❖ 8-ounce crumbled, cooked bacon
- ❖ 4 eggs
- ❖ Two c. milk

## Instructions:

i.   Mix the eggs, salt, and milk in a blender. Mix in the flour. Fold in the bacon and herbs and rest for an hour.

ii.  Add wood pellets to your smoker and follow your cooker's startup procedure. Preheat your smoker, with your lid closed, until it reaches 400.

iii. Place the muffin tin on the grill to heat up. Once hot, quickly add a t. of butter to each cavity. Fill to almost full with the batter. Grill for another 15 minutes. Turn the heat to 350, and cook for 20 minutes. Don't open the grill while cooking.

iv.  Serve.

**Servings| 8-12**                          **Time required: 1.5 hour**

# Bacon-Wrapped Chestnuts

## *Ingredients:*

- ❖ 1/3 c. barbecue sauce
- ❖ Two 8-ounce cans whole water chestnuts
- ❖ 1/3 c. mayonnaise
- ❖ 1/3 c. brown sugar
- ❖ One pound bacon

## *Instructions:*

i.   Add wood pellets to your smoker and follow your cooker's startup procedure. Preheat your smoker, with your lid closed, until it reaches 350.

ii.  Cut the bacon in half and wrap around the nuts. Use a toothpick to secure.

iii. Lay them on a baking sheet and lay the baking sheet on the grill. Allow them to smoke for 20 minutes.

iv.  Mix the mayo, barbecue sauce, and brown sugar together. Pour this over the chestnuts and bake for another 10-15 minutes.

v.   Serve.

**Servings| 6-8**              **Time required: 45 minutes**

# Bacon Onion Rings

## *Ingredients:*

- ❖ One t. honey
- ❖ One T. mustard
- ❖ Two large onions, sliced ½-inch thick
- ❖ One package bacon
- ❖ One T. chili garlic sauce

## *Instructions:*

i.   Wrap the bacon around the individual onion rings. Do this until you run out of bacon. Use a skewer to keep the bacon from unwrapping.

ii.  Add wood pellets to your smoker and follow your cooker's startup procedure. Preheat your smoker, with your lid closed, until it reaches 400.

iii. For 90 minutes, grill the onions. Turn halfway through.

iv.  Mix the remaining ingredients together and serve with the onion rings.

**Servings| 6-8**          **Time required: 1.5 hours**

# Apple Crisp

## *Ingredients:*

- ❖ One T. maple syrup
- ❖ Two T. pecan chips
- ❖ ½ stick butter
- ❖ One T. pumpkin pie spice
- ❖ 1 ½ T brown sugar
- ❖ Craisins
- ❖ ½ c. granola
- ❖ lemon juice
- ❖ 3 apples

## *Instructions:*

i.    Add wood pellets to your smoker and follow your cooker's startup procedure. Preheat your smoker, with your lid closed, until it reaches 400.

ii.   Wash the apples, slice in half, and remove the core. Slice a bit off the back so that they lay flat. Place on a tray.

iii.  Mix the remaining ingredients together. Divide the granola between the apple halves. Allow this to grill for 30 minutes.

iv.   Pairs well with vanilla ice cream.

**Servings| 6**              **Time required: 45 minutes**

Made in the USA
Lexington, KY
31 May 2019